THE SECOND TREASURY OF CONTEMPORARY HOUSES

THE SECOND TREASURY OF CONTEMPORARY HOUSES

Selected by the Editors of Architectural Record

Published by F. W. Dodge Corporation

FOREWORD

American house design is being impressed on us today as probably never before. All our mass communications media constantly beguile us with the latest ideas, gimmicks, and colors. This attention follows the much-talked-about pattern of increased interest in all the arts. Are the architectural results good or bad? Perhaps the most interesting answer to this is the reaction of the rest of the world.

Only a short while ago, others admitted our superiority in "plumbing," but reserved to themselves the lead in building qualities for "good living." Many here agreed. Now, the United States has suddenly become a Mecca to which laymen, as well as architects, come to see and study good domestic architecture. The fact that they come in increasing numbers seems evidence that a more matured architectural creativity is developing here.

Yet they find all kinds of new houses. We still have the enormous variety in house design that Emerson Goble, Editor of Architectural Record, noted in his introduction to our first collection, A Treasury of Contemporary Houses, in 1954. Some architects have dubbed the current varied state of architectural affairs as "the new freedom" in design. Some laud, some decry this diversity — generally with each following his own bent. But, *at the least, from this designers' freedom of expression, home-owners have a vast freedom of choice to satisfy their own tastes in contemporary houses.*

This book reflects that wide variety. It has been our task for the past few years to search carefully through the myriads of houses built to find the very best we could of each trend or style. The twenty or so most significant contemporary ones have been published annually as "Record Houses" by Architectural Record. From among these were selected the houses presented in this book. They form, we believe, a good cross section of the recent work of outstanding architects throughout the country. They are of all types, sizes, and costs.

On the subject of costs — at a recent radio interview where some of these houses were discussed, the question was posed: "But don't architect-designed houses cost more?" Some general reasons to the contrary were advanced, notably the assurance of sound, lasting value in what is the largest single investment made by most families. And, of course, there is the fact that many skilled architects serve the low-cost builder-house and prefabricated-house fields. (There are some builder houses in this book.) It was only after the interview, though — as so often happens — that a quotation was recalled that sums up what dollars spent for good architecture really buy. It is from a 1943 speech of Winston Churchill's: "We shape our buildings, and afterwards our buildings shape us."

Thus we offer this selection of houses in the spirit with which George Bain Cummings, then President of the American Institute of Architects, generously launched our "Record Houses" program in 1956: "Here [one] may observe evidence of easier, healthier, safer, and more enjoyable living through architecture."

HERBERT L. SMITH JR.
Associate Editor
Architectural Record

CONTENTS

HOUSES AND PEOPLE

EAST

NORTH-CENTRAL

SOUTH

WEST

INDEX

HOUSES AND PEOPLE

THE AMERICAN AT HOME

BY RUSSELL LYNES *

"I WONDER," a friend said to me recently, "if the modern house, so open, so transparent, so free from dark corners and hiding places and secrets doesn't reflect the influence of psychiatry on our generation."

I was reminded by this of what one of the most articulate of all American writers on architecture, Andrew Jackson Downing, said a little more than a century ago as he looked about him at the houses that his contemporaries were building in the 1840s. "Much of the character of everyman," he wrote, "may be read in his house."

I have just been thumbing through the paste-ups of the pages of houses that make up this volume and I have been trying to read the character of "everyman" in them. Even in their freshness they are full of echoes from Mr. Downing's day and before; the character of the frontier American speaks through them just as clearly as the character of the "organization man." The desire for individuality that so puzzled visitors to America in the 1830s because it was so vocal and yet so coupled with belief in conformity is still here. But in many ways it is apparent that the American family has changed and that its aspirations are not what they once were.

Another nineteenth century man who, like Downing, wrote about architecture was the phrenologist O. S. Fowler, who started the cult for the octagonal house. "Beautiful birds build tasty nests," he said. ". . . a fancy man will build a fancy cottage, a practical man, a convenient house; a substantial man, a solid edifice; a weak man, an illy arranged house; an aspiring man a high house, and a superior man, a superb villa."

I do not intend to practice phrenology on the individual houses that are reproduced here. They are all in their different ways "tasty nests." But I should like to try to draw from their characteristics some generalizations about how America is changing and how it stays the same.

The most striking, and possibly the most obvious, generalization that one can draw is that one of the traditions of American domestic architecture has disappeared. We have given up what was once a strong desire of many American families to build for permanence, to establish a family seat which might serve a succession of generations. Several years ago I laughed when the artist Robert Osborn told me that he had engaged a young architect to build a studio for him in Salisbury, Connecticut, and had told him he wanted it made of brick. The young architect refused. "Brick is too permanent," he said. It sounds odd, but it is a reflection of a state of mind that we cannot dismiss. He had a valid point, even if Mr. Osborn hired another architect. The client, after all, has a right to think brick is pretty.

The other most important characteristic revealed by the houses herein, as I see it, is one that you may quarrel with. We are returning to a basic kind of American architecture that one would have thought we had discarded. The new architecture is a frontier architecture, an architecture built as much to move out of as to move into. The American house has become a stepping stone. It has become a stop on an incessant journey. Indeed some of the houses seem to be in motion themselves, hovering just above the ground, not on it, as though they might flap their wings and migrate at any moment.

Recently, I visited in Richmond and spent many hours looking at the great plantation houses built on the banks of the James River. I was lucky enough to have lunch at Westover, but I arrived there early, too soon to ring the doorbell, and I spent an hour wandering through the gardens where snow was on the box bushes and cardinals and bluebirds (this was in January) perched in naked fruit trees. I looked at the house from the river side, its true façade but not the one one sees first, a house of tremendous elegance — perhaps, I thought, the most splendid piece of domestic architecture in America. I looked at the barns and outbuildings built, like the main house, of brick and at the circular privy with a fireplace and windows and facilities for a family of five. This, I thought, must have been the origin of "togetherness" which we seem to have rediscovered in another context. Americans were, to be sure, less prudish in the eighteenth century than they are now.

Westover represents the vanishing idea of the house built for the great grandchildren. "I have settled here," it seems to say, "and I mean to stay here. I am not just a building, I am the monument to a permanent philosophy of the good life." The way of life that Colonel William Byrd II built into his splendid Georgian mansion, a rather despotic life but one in which culture

* Mr. Lynes is Managing Editor of Harper's Magazine and is author of such books as The Tastemakers; Snobs; Guests; A Surfeit of Honey; and Highbrow, Lowbrow, Middlebrow.

and education and a knowledge of the world were insisted upon, lasted from about 1730 until the Civil War, when the library wing was burned. (The library happily had been removed and the wing has been adequately if not perfectly replaced.) The echo of the way of life is still there, and one cannot help but hear it. But it is an echo from Europe, not only architecturally but in its sureness that a permanent class structure could be taken for granted, that there would always be a landed gentry and a cultured upper class of limited size but almost unlimited power. Indeed one still hears talk of this sort in Virginia, but it is filled with nostalgia and lacks the ring of conviction.

The Civil War by no means did away with the concept of building for future generations; it merely shifted the location from the South to the North, and from an agricultural aristocracy to a new industrial and financial society. The splendid house set in thousands of acres of cultivated land lingered, but in poverty, and the great princely palace from which its overseer sallied forth into the world of financial conflict became the new family seat. Colonel Colt, who invented the revolver that bears his name, elected to build himself a villa in Hartford, part Italian and part Turkish, with towers and minarets and glass domes. A little later, when Richard Morris Hunt became America's foremost domestic architect, he built massive chateaux for the Vanderbilts and marble palaces (which were called "cottages") for the Goelets and the Astors and still more Vanderbilts at Newport. They were constructed to stand as their prototypes in Europe had already stood for centuries, and the dates of their erection were carved over the doorways for future centuries to look upon with awe.

And now they are gone, most of them. Gone, that is, as houses. Some, like "The Breakers" at Newport and "Biltmore" in Ashville, are museums open to the public — many others are now schools or convents or recreation centers for the employes of large corporations.

The fact is that America's several conscientious efforts to establish permanent domestic architecture have failed, and if this is a matter of small moment to us today, the reasons for it explain a great deal about why we live in the kinds of houses we do and why domestic architecture today goes in the directions it does.

We were trying to superimpose on a highly mobile society the architecture of a comparably static society. In Europe, where there had long been (and still is) a rigid class structure, a man and his family "knew its place" and for the most part was content to remain within its class. The principal building material was stone, and a house built in the fourteenth century was still, with renovations, habitable in the twentieth. Families stayed put, for the most part, in the village or city in which their forebears had lived; continuity

"We have given up . . .

"Armsmere," home of Col. Samuel Colt, Hartford, Conn.

The New York Historical Society

Home and laboratory of G. G. Green, Woodbury, N. J.

a strong desire . . . to establish a family seat."

RUSSELL LYNES

"Olana," home of Frederick Church, Hudson, N. Y.

A New Jersey bungalow

RUSSELL LYNES

"We are returning to . . . an architecture built as much to move out of as to move into."

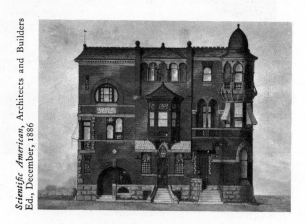

Scientific American, Architects and Builders Ed., December, 1886

Scientific American, Architects and Builders Ed., December, 1887

was important, possibly because there was nowhere to go but overseas, and those who went to the colonies (unless they migrated permanently) always considered the place they had come from as the place they would ultimately go back to. "It's a Long, Long Way to Tipperary," was the British song of World War I. Ours was "How You Gonna Keep 'em Down on the Farm, after they've seen Paree?"

The American's attitude towards his home was quite different. Home, so long as he was on his native soil, was where he was as much as where he had come from; no home was so dear to his heart that he hesitated to leave if he could discover one he thought would be better. The society in which he lived and the American dream which guided his ambition were, he believed, always beckoning him forward. It did not occur to him that he was stuck in any special social class, and that if he were ingenious enough, lucky enough, and adventurous enough he could not escape from his surroundings into more palatable ones. Some men believed they could better their lot with their backs in the wilderness, some that they could push forward with their brains in the universities, or with their wits in the market place, but however many resigned themselves to staying put, there were always spectacular examples of those who moved on, some to catastrophe and some to astonishing success.

How do you house such a mobile society? You house it in temporary buildings, or buildings, anyway, that you would like to think will not become slums . . . buildings that should be, even if they are not, torn down after a generation.

It seems to me interesting, now that there are no more real physical frontiers in America, that it should be the architecture of impermanence that has won out. The architecture of the economic, spiritual, and social frontier has replaced the architecture of the physical frontier.

Look for example at what happens to the typical family. The chronological sequence from matrimony to retirement goes something like this — the new family starts life in an urban housing development or possibly in a small flat in a remodeled brownstone house or an apartment over a store. But soon there are children and the itch comes to get into one of the less expensive, mass-produced suburbs, a Levittown of some sort, and the young family buys a house. It doesn't, however, do so with any intention of staying there. It is merely a stepping stone to another kind of suburban community where the houses are less like cubes taken from the same box of sugar, a development in which the ranch houses are set somewhat differently on the land and painted in different colors. But this, too, is only a step towards another kind of community with more land and more trees and a bigger house even less like its neighbor, perhaps in one of the "older and better established" suburbs. By now what was our young couple may be in their fifties and one would think that they had settled down. But no, the children have grown up, married and set up households of their own; the couple no longer need as much room as they once did and they hope soon to retire, to give up the commuter's life and the rigors of competition, and buy a nice little house somewhere where it is warm all year, in California, perhaps, or Arizona or Florida. In the course of their marriage, then, they have lived in half a dozen places, each one a stop on the way to some place else. They have been continually on the economic, spiritual, and social frontier.

We are, taken as a whole, more used to change than to permanence. When we build a house or buy one the least of our concerns is whether the next generation of our family will want to make it their home. We don't expect anyone to make a family seat out of a Hardoy chair. But changes come so fast in American life that we are scarcely aware of how far reaching they are. It would take a book (indeed I recently took a book) to outline the changes in our society in the last decade, but look with me for a moment at a few of the changes in our manners and customs that are, or will be, reflected in our houses.

The young marry younger than they used to a few decades ago, and they have more children (oblivious of the fact that the growth of our population is one of the greatest headaches that their generation is going to have to face). Many young marriages now are consummated in college, and universities are having to provide housing facilities for young couples. Teenagers, traditionally promiscuous, are becoming monogamous. The convention of "going steady" threatens to change the sexual mores of the nation, and there are those who believe that going steady will result in an alarming increase in the divorce rate which has already become alarming because of so many immature marriages. Women are assuming jobs and responsibilities that we have long thought were the prerogatives of men, and men are in their turn taking on a good many chores that a generation ago would have seemed preposterous as man's work. Shorter working hours mean that more Americans are at home more of the time than they used to be. On the other hand mother is out of the house a great deal more than her mother was. She is on the road to the supermarket, the station, the school, the church, the PTA, and in many cases she is at her office from nine to five.

This is only a small part of the picture of change. With the shortage of domestic servants life has become more informal. With the reversal in the cultural (with a small "c") trade winds (they now blow from California to the east) Americans everywhere have taken to the out of doors, to the barbecue pit and the patio, and to dressing themselves in perpetual variations on beachwear. The suburbs where the outdoor life is pursued have assumed a place in our national pattern of living that has not only antiquated our transportation systems and local governments, but has threatened to become a brand new kind of social simplex (as opposed to complex) in which, as I have suggested, there is no place to rise; the only way up is out. Soon it will be a question of where one can go that is out. Cities are no longer self-contained units dotted on the map; they run from one into another. As Christopher Tunnard of Yale has noted, the strip down the eastern coast from Maine to the District of Columbia is one unbroken urban area.

As our lives become more cluttered and our neighbors closer we hear a great deal about "mass"-this and "mass"-that — about mass-culture and mass-communications and mass-media and mass-housing and, of course, about mass-production. We hear less about the struggle for individuality, which goes on as usual, and about the non-conformists who are, I suspect, around in just about the same ratio as they have always been. They are neither so noticeable nor so vocal in periods of prosperity as they are when there is dissatisfaction, but those who raise their voices are looked upon with just about as much suspicion by conformists as they have been since the beginning of the Christian era. They may be pilloried, some of them, but at least we don't remove their skins or break them on wheels or feed them to lions.

If we did, the houses that are illustrated in this volume, would not, of course, have been built. They surely do not conform to any mass-production standards of taste, and they are (there is no reason not to admit) outlandish to a great many good and useful people. They are a new kind of frontier architecture.

But against this background of change, conformity, and revolt that I have barely sketched, what, in Mr. Downing's words, can we read of the character of everyman in his house?

From the point of view of even a casual observer of the idiosyncrasies of social behavior like myself, nothing is more useful than a group of brand-new houses that do not slavishly conform to traditional patterns. They epitomize, without the curtains of tradition to obscure them, the most up-to-date aspirations of the family and the ways in which it believes these aspirations for the good life can be practically realized. In a very real sense every good architect is a practicing social scientist. He measures, gauges, and reduces to a formula the social unit for which he is designing, and the formula that he produces (sometimes more "elegant," in the scientist's meaning of the word, than at other times) is a building. What generalities can we discover by applying his formula to the American at home today?

First, let's look at the children, for this takes us back to the beginning of this essay and the friend who wondered about the influence of psychiatry on the modern home. There is a tendency in the modern house to return to the nineteenth-century practice of isolating the children from the rest of the house, to establish in effect what was once thought of in large mansions as the children's wing. But the children no longer have bedrooms which are also playrooms; they have pigeon holes for sleeping and a play area which someday, it is hoped, they will use for teenage riotous living off there somewhere out of earshot. They are given a place where they can make a mess that will not make a mess of the rest of the house, where they can "express" themselves to their little hearts' content. They are, you might say, provided for, but as Lewis Mumford has written, "the numerous nooks and hiding places, dear to children . . . nooks that gave the young places for quiet dreaming and mischievous eavesdropping on their elders," have gone. Such a statement seems rather sentimental and old-fashioned when we look at the modern house, but it is a fact nonetheless and a reflection of our attitude towards the psyche of the child. We believe in the open mind, in the open plan, in the importance of the facts of life and not of the myths of childhood. In some respects we have given Freud a long white beard and a red cap and made him into Santa Claus. If we are good, he will bring us adjustment for Christmas.

I would not say that this was not healthy. What we are doing instead of turning the children over to Nanny to discipline and amuse and produce at the children's hour, is to provide them with safe isolation where, at the same time, they can be observed. Now that we are returning to the nineteenth-century ideal of the large family we have to provide a place for the children that is not directly underfoot. It is interesting in this context that while the size of the family increases so do the complaints of many young housewives that there are too many demands on their time. It would, I suppose, be unfair to say that they create the demands so that they can make the complaints, but it sometimes seems that way.

The nineteenth century keeps coming to mind as one considers the houses in this issue. The "family room" has in many houses taken the place of the living room, and it seems to mean that the kitchen has become the center of life as it once was in the farmhouse. The kitchen has in some cases grown in space and in function; in other cases it is an adjunct of the living room in order, presumably, that mother does not have to suffer from isolation. This, apparently, indicates that mother again wants to cook and not merely to heat up frozen or canned foods. Cooking has regained its place as a creative function, an opportunity for self-expression, and an exercise in "togetherness." It hints at the reversal of a trend: women are becoming more womanly, which will be a relief to a great many men.

Mansard House, Hudson, N. Y.

"Verandas, piazzas, bay windows, balconies, etc., are the most valuable general truths of domestic architecture."

RUSSELL LYNES
Gothic Revival house, Hudson, N. Y.

RUSSELL LYNES
Browne Funeral Home, Thompson, Conn.

An old home made new, Chicago, Ill.

RUSSELL LYNES

Home of John Cox Stevens, Hoboken, N. J.

Metropolitan Museum of Art

"The façade . . . is disappearing . . ."

Scientific American, Architects and Builders
Ed., June, 1887

In this connection one cannot but be impressed with the smallness of bedrooms in comparison to "family rooms." The bedroom is now precisely that and nothing more. (Dorothy Parker once said of a tiny office that she was sharing with Robert Benchley, "If this room were six inches smaller in any dimension this would be adultery.") The function of the bedroom has been recognized for what it is rather than what it was in the days when it was a place to loll, a place where a woman could write at her desk in her nightie, or sit by the window and sew, a place to paddle around with hair down and face covered with cold cream without the sense, as one must have in the family room, that one is facing the world. The boudoir is gone. Too bad. When the kitchen and the bedroom become adjuncts of the family room something has been lost even if something has been gained.

But let's turn our attention to the house as a whole for a minute. Downing wrote in *The Architecture of Country Houses*, "Verandas, piazzas, bay-windows, balconies, etc., are the most valuable general truths of Domestic Architecture." They were all important in the mid-nineteenth-century house, but when we got involved in adaptations of French chateaux and cute little Dutch houses and revivals of colonial homes and "salt boxes," as we did in the earlier part of this century, they all but disappeared. We are now recognizing again the general truths that Mr. Downing thought so important. We have substituted the screened porch and the patio for the verandas and piazzas, sheltered places to sit out of doors, and we have introduced the indoor garden for the glassed-in solarium. The bay window is now a glass wall that gives us the same sense of being indoors and out at the same time. Balconies are now standard equipment of new apartment houses, and though rural or suburban houses no longer have them very often, roofs are not infrequently made into sun decks which serve the same purpose.

But if Mr. Downing's ideas persist, there are others evident in the houses in this issue that would surprise him, and that would tell him how America has changed. The façade, for example, is disappearing and the house, instead of being an interruption in the landscape or an accent in it, has become merely a piece of landscape enclosed for purposes of shelter. The denial of the façade could be interpreted as unneighborly, a turning of the back, but only in the sense that it flouts a convention that most people respect. In some cases, of course, the modern house simply excludes the neighbors with a high stonewall, and in these cases the architect, as I interpret it, is attempting to provide the kind of privacy that once could be achieved only by a house on many acres of land. If a house is going to be transparent, then its privacy must be protected, though once you are permitted inside the wall, the house is an open book . . . a gesture of friendliness almost beyond the call of duty. In some other respects the house behind the wall is very like the nineteenth-century manor house set at the end of a long driveway. It bespeaks not only desire for privacy but for social exclusiveness.

The concern with clutching the outdoors within walls and with gardens inside the house, speaks, of course, of the urbanization of our society. In the days when men worked out of doors, houses were built to shut away the elements, to keep nature in its place, sometimes enemy, sometimes friend, but always something that had to be coped with. In the modern house nature is a permanent guest. It is also, of course, a substitute for architectural ornament, a means of achieving variety without having to invent it, of softening without seeming to be a softy, of stopping the eye as it slides over a smooth surface without violating any architectural doctrines. It often seems to be an answer to the house rather than an extension of it, just as a "playful use of materials" seems to be a way around the problem of dullness rather than a head-on assault on how to provide delight for the eye.

I think that you will discover, if you will look at the plans and photographs of the houses in this book, that convenience has in some cases been sacrificed to appearance. You will find that it is occasionally necessary to go out of doors to get from bedroom to living room, for example. You will find space, as we've noted, cut to the minimum in the bedroom in order to provide a more spacious effect somewhere else. You will find a great many plants to be watered and leaves to be wiped. You will even find a hint that the "parlor," so long in the doldrums, is being revived. Perhaps nothing about these houses tells us more about the families for whom they were built than this.

It tells us that they are not trying to live entirely rational lives in entirely rational surroundings. It means that they are no longer the creatures of functionalism and that they are aware that there are conveniences of the flesh that are worth foregoing for pleasures of the spirit. It means that they have struck a blow for eccentricity and experiment, by trying to reorder their lives in such a manner that the machinery of life does not dictate and circumscribe the fun of life. A good thing.

But it is well to remember that the people who have paid for these houses are relatively free spirits or they would not have invested their hearts and their bank accounts in this particular kind of frontier architecture — an architecture on a new kind of frontier, a frontier of time.

We are just beginning to discover what this new frontier is. The sociology department of the University of Chicago is studying it. The Twentieth Century Fund is about to launch into an investigation of it. Magazine editors are feeling their way into parts of it, a foray here and a scouting party there. It is the frontier of leisure, the rapidly expanding void of time that threatens to engulf us. The twenty-eight-hour week and the three-day weekend. There is almost no one who doesn't think it would be good to have more leisure time, but there is an increasing number of thoughtful people who wonder what it will do to family life, to our culture, to education and to peace of mind. What can be done to make leisure productive? (This is the Puritan point of view.) What can be done to make it satisfying and not stultifying? What will it do to our highways, our national parks, our public beaches? What will it do to our houses?

One of the answers, I believe, is to be found in this presentation. It will change the looks of our houses, just as these buildings are already changed from traditional patterns that date back to the sixty-hour week. It will make the house into a new kind of recreation center in which the needs of every member of the family are reconsidered in the light of the new leisure. It will be housing for the intentionally part-time unemployed in a country crowded with people who do their own domestic work, who live on relatively small pieces of land in areas that are far more urban than rural, who want to be private but at the same time identified with the community, who want the sun and light by day and protection from the dark by night.

I would not, since I am no more crystal-gazer than phrenologist, attempt to forecast what the new leisure will do to the design of houses, any more than I am willing to guess what it will do to the shape and flavor of the typical American family. But we can glimpse, I believe, what may happen by looking at houses designed by those architects who are trying to cope with the first hints of this problem, with its obvious benefits as well as with its more subtle threats.

The architecture of mass leisure, if I read the clues correctly, will have a kind of adaptability that assures privacy when it is wanted, congregation in "family rooms" and segregation when the members of the family get to be too much for one another. It will be flexible so that some rooms will come and go as needed, just as the outdoors will come and go. The kitchen may become a place that mother will be happy to retire to, if she has her husband around so much of the time, or it may become the center of family activity. In other words, the house of the new era of leisure will attempt to do in a small space what the great house of the eighteenth century, like Westover, or the villa of the nineteenth century, accomplished by the use of lavish space: provide a relaxed setting for a life of busy leisure.

But of one thing I think we may be reasonably sure. The American architecture of leisure will have no illusions of permanence. However tasty the nests, the horizon will always beckon and the beautiful birds will be forever in search of some new and unsuspected frontier.

"American Country Life, May Morning,"
Currier & Ives, 1855

*"Americans have taken . . . to the barbeque
pits and the patios."*

"Home from the Brook," Currier & Ives, 1867

"The suburbs . . . a brand new kind of social simplex"

Bay Ridge, Long Island, 1860, from the
J. Clarence Davies Collection

*"The rapidly expanding void of time . . .
will make the house into a new kind of recreation
center . . ."*

Great Republic steamboat cabin

ULRICH FRANZEN, ARCHITECT AND OWNER.   RAYBECK INC., CONTRACTOR

THE NEW HOUSE FOR FAMILY LIVING

By A. Lawrence Kocher

"It is among the conditions of a true Architecture that it mould itself to the wants and the domestic habits and the public customs and the political institutions and the religious sentiment of its country and its age; that it assort with the materials on hand, submitting to modifications as new materials present themselves; and that it avail itself, from time to time, of the various aids which mathematical and mechanical and chemical science offer, for its convenience and advancement."
Robert Dale Owen, Smithsonian Institution, in *Hints on Public Architecture*. N. Y., 1849

THE JUDGMENT of what is considered significant in the field of house design, at a given moment, must necessarily be qualified and approximate. Esthetic judgment, it seems to us, is usually divided and errant. Some of us, by nature, have a fixed classical strain, due to inheritance or training, while others, in an opposite camp, will favor nothing but what is new and exploratory. It is our intention here, to select a number of houses that represent a contribution to our fund of knowledge of how the house—the American house of today—should be planned, constructed, and outwardly enclosed. Our chief interest is not solely with the propagation of ideas of favorite appearance but rather with the solution of current problems of planning and design fitness.

The houses that we have chosen for illustration and discussion in these pages, constitute, we believe, a distinguished anthology of contemporary

ARCHITECTURAL PHOTOGRAPHS © EZRA STOLLER   FAMILY PHOTOGRAPHS BY ELLIOT ERWITT — MAGNUM

domestic architecture. The examples are, in a sense, a summary of outstanding houses built by architects of the U.S.A. during the past few years. Creative effort, such as is required in designing a successful dwelling, public building, or shaping a community, is an accomplishment that is deserving of thoughtful evaluation and public notice.

A House That Is Lived In

We have chosen, in this presentation, to break with tradition in architectural publication, by showing one of our selected houses as occupied by a family. Our illustrations are of its living, dining, and play areas, in actual use. The Ulrich Franzens, who developed and built the house, were photographed with the interior as a background. They appear as normally concerned with routine activities; caring for children, preparation of food, dining, entertaining guests, and relaxing.

Mr. Franzen is an architect, Harvard trained, whose ideas for the house were supported and aided by his wife, a Bennington College graduate. The two spent several months in setting up space needs for their family of three children (a girl and two boys) plus a dog and a cat.

The design objective was to create a house for their particular family, one that gave promise of lasting usefulness and attraction. "Not a place,"

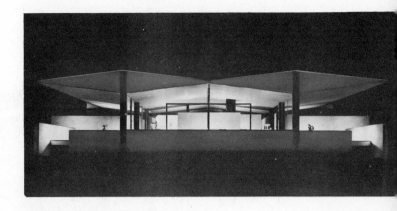

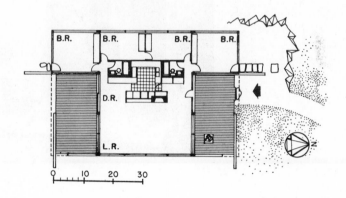

observed Mrs. Franzen, "that was sterile of ideas, soon to be outmoded and outlived — soon to become the *nightmare*, as to 'The Man in the Gray Flannel Suit'." It was a requirement of the plan that there be space throughout the house, for the effective display of a varied collection of contemporary art, consisting of murals, small paintings and sculpture.

The site was selected after a long search by auto excursions into three states bordering New York City, where the architect has his office. The two-acre plot, on which the house is placed, is thickly wooded and has rugged outcroppings of stone. An ancient stone wall borders one side of the property. Because of the nature of the ground and a preference for the natural setting, there was no need for formal planting and an expanse of lawn, difficult to maintain.

The house is two miles from the town of Rye, New York, and three-quarters of an hour commuting time from Manhattan. There are nursery and public schools nearby; a bathing beach and boat basin on Long Island Sound are within a short walking distance.

We consider the Franzen house, shown on these opening pages, to be a fair example of the sort of domestic design that is being contrived today by an enthusiastic group of young architects whose training, since the Second World War, has stressed and applied the theoretical and experi-

A very new and different approach to planning a house has been used by architect Ulrich J. Franzen in his home for his own family. Light diamond-shaped trusses soar over a very free and unobstructed "platform for living." The roof is supported by eight columns, and interior partitions are low, free-standing. The house is delightful to look at, interesting to study.

But what is it like to live in? To find out, the editors of ARCHITECTURAL RECORD *spent a day with the Franzen family. These photos are the result.*

"The buildings of a country and an age should be ethnological expressions of the wants, habits, arts, and feelings of the time in which they were erected."
JOSEPH HENRY, WRITINGS, 1856

The kitchen is the central hub of the Franzen house; actually in the middle of the house, it is, nevertheless, flooded with daylight over low partitions and storage walls, and from the long, narrow skylight which bisects the ceiling. The kitchen can be closed-off, but open, it permits Mrs. Franzen a close association with the family. Both terraces, children's bedrooms and playroom are easily supervised from the area. Two bathrooms flank the kitchen to form a unified mechanical core. The baths have ceilings at partition height.

"Architecture must possess a certain flexibility. Its external forms must not control and dictate its internal adaptations."

R. D. OWEN, 1848

mental. The nature of its light steel roof framing, the manner in which the outer enclosing walls and inner partitions are completely independent of the structural frame, the wide selection of factory fabricated units, along with large sheets of plate glass and insulation panels — all make us aware of a new approach to design and a skillfully contrived shaping of construction. Industrial production, as here, is playing an increasing part in current efforts by architects of energy and creative ambition.

The house as architecture has a quality that is quite different from that to which we have long been accustomed, looking back a decade or more. We must admit that occasionally we are startled by its daring, but, at the same time, vastly stimulated by the courageous effort that is being exerted in order to avoid any semblance of the century-long practice of copying ideas of others or style borrowing from the past. We can fittingly quote Gauguin here, who said that in art there are only revolutionists and plagiarists. If architects at this moment are appearing to be in revolt, it is with a sense of gain for the future, since all movements that have taken place in the past for the improvement of architecture, have been preceded by revolt.

Future art historians will probably speak of the mid-decades of the

Outdoor living is well provided for in the Franzen house. The roof spreads over terraces on either side of the house, providing sunny or shaded areas, morning or evening, as desired. Glass walls slide open to link terraces with living area in fine weather. Visually, terraces form part of the room at all times. A small basement for storage and heating plant is reached through a trap door (photo far right). Floors are red oak, ceilings fir boarding. Insects are controlled by spraying the grounds, which seems successful.

"It is only when a building expresses the dominant sentiment of an age . . . that it is entitled to our admiration."

JOSEPH HENRY, WRITINGS 1856

twentieth century as a time of artistic rebellion and change. It is now, during these years, that we have come to accept change and disown our artistic inheritance. We try to avoid the stigma of being considered traditional or followers of the cliché. The old stylistic standards which for centuries were the measuring stick for judging architecture are at this time definitely neglected or outmoded. That architect is an exceptional rarity who would suggest to a client that a proposed house for an American suburb be given a colonial, Spanish or French provincial look. Even the current ranch house rage can be considered a cloak covering a free-flowing, if emaciated, non-stylistic manner. A dissenting architect called it "modern in sheep-ranch clothing!"

Age of Experimentation

In the face of this recognized design upheaval, it is natural that we look for the causes. A part of the origin of the upheaval — some would call it a revolution — can be traced to a chastening influence of the depression of the thirties. We see plainly a decline in the century-long domination of "style" taking place gradually as a consequence of stringent conditions during the early depression years. There was an extreme necessity for economy at the time. Housing was an urgent need, yet

almost none was provided. In order to cut costs, building forms were greatly simplified; elaborate doorways, denticulated cornices and Spanish ironwork were banished from domestic work. Among the mementoes of these years were a country wide rash of Tom Thumb Golf courses and the equally widespread Drive-in Overnight Cabins — forerunners of the deluxe Motels of today. These stimulants to recovery were not jobs for the architect, even though they represented our single, but brief, building boom. Architects, during the lull, became interested in low cost housing; some dabbled in prefabrication. Experimentation was taking place by both architects and industry. New materials and novel construction methods were turned to as a means of cutting costs. Among the new materials introduced were fiber and pressboards, plywood (quantity produced), asbestos-cement products, plastics of an early kind, aluminum and other metals. Houses with steel frame, faced with panels of standard widths, others of plywood, canvas surfaced, precast concrete units and porcelain enameled steel walls were announced for marketing, although almost none reached a mass production stage. These happenings were among the evidences of a disrupted architectural practice.

A second cause leading to change in the nature and aims of architectural practice, can be attributed to altered teaching methods of archi-

tectural schools. The use of the Orders of Architecture as the *vade mecum* for imparting good proportion and a vocabulary of architecture, was gradually given up. Most of the accredited schools ceased to bend the knee or do homage to the Ecole des Beaux Arts in Paris. Back in 1924 George Bernard Shaw, in a letter to ARCHITECTURAL RECORD in response to a questionnaire concerning the training of the architect, anticipated the coming change in teaching when he said tartly that

> "Architects are made by building, not by books . . . that
> the more an architect knows academically, the worse he builds.
> Reading, picture-gazing, and globe trotting all tend to shift
> an architect's eyes to the back of his head."

At the height of the so-called teaching change, shortly after 1936, Walter Gropius, a distinguished teacher and founder of the German Bauhaus, was brought to Harvard and placed in charge of courses in the school of design. He soon attracted to this country his Bauhaus aides, Mies van der Rohe, Joseph Albers, Marcel Breuer, Herbert Bayer, Howard Dearstyne and L. Moholy-Nagy. All of these Bauhaus associates, without exception, found places in architectural schools. They, with many others in the profession, were to turn the attention of America to

one of our most fruitful and typical resources, namely mass production and standardization. We may hesitate to accept the utilitarian Ford factory and the supermarket villages as possessing esthetic qualities, but we can welcome the clear evidences of arrival at a freer, more original and imaginative interpretation of the house as it is being experimentally produced today for American family living.

Current Trends in House Design

As we leaf over the accompanying pages to form a preliminary impression of current offerings in house design, we become aware that the long-familiar oversized and traditional *country house*, set back from the limits of the property, usually alongside a formal garden, is now seemingly obsolete. Increased building costs and taxation have taken care of that. Houses built now are manifestly suburban and informal in character. They are far less pretentious and extravagant; more significantly, they are outwardly a logical expression of our industrial age and of our American manner of living.

The contemporary house has a "new look." It consists of a more open grouping of rooms, usually all on one floor. Its facing of masonry and weatherboarding has been largely replaced by the window wall, and, in

The open plan of the living area in the Franzen house lends itself well to entertaining large groups, as (photos at left) when the Franzens were visited by RECORD *editors and the Arthur Murray family. Free-standing canvas panels break the room into several conversation areas, and serve as display panels for paintings and murals. The fireplace is inset and flanked by an alcove for display of art objects, lighted from above.*

"A house whose inside is as open and manifest as a bird's nest . . . where to be a guest is to be presented with the freedom of the house, and not to be excluded from seven-eighths of it, shut up in a particular cell, and told to make yourself at home there, — in solitary confinement."

HENRY D. THOREAU, WALDEN

some instances, by a complete encirclement of glass. In addition, a new system of fabrication is being introduced which makes use of a steel or wood framework, and has an infilling of glass or factory-made panels. It is obvious from our illustrations that the architect of today has become more daring, and more, what we may term, "industrial minded"; his methods of construction are more technical and complicated than a generation ago. Newer building operations require a close partnership of architect, engineer and industry. The combination of steel, glass, plastics and other materials make it urgently necessary that all parts be fitted together as a delicate and complex mechanism.

Returning to our review of current houses, we can perceive here and there, the novelty of a frankly revealed structural skeleton. Vertical supports on the surface of the house are modularly spaced with a regularity that produces a pleasant wall pattern similar to the outer facing of a Japanese house. There is, as we know from oriental examples, an esthetic attraction in a revealed structure. Mies van der Rohe, who applies this system for dwellings, has succeeded in creating wall units that are attractive by their patterning and rhythm. August Perret in France has, of course, been using reinforced concrete as the bare bones

of his buildings since 1900, with interstices filled with concrete or brick.

Partitions within the house have been undergoing a transformation of purpose. Instead of being rigidly fixed and supporting, they are now often flexible and movable to a new location. They sometimes extend upward to a height not exceeding an easy reach, that is, just above the sight lines. Closets, that are organized, with subdivisions for trays, racks, shelves and hanging rods, are occasionally installed as a means for subdividing, either temporarily or permanently, the entire area of a house floor. Freestanding walls are often placed at right angles to one another. Their function is largely non-structural—they may, as in the Franzen house, serve as a termination of a terrace, producing a subdivision in the adjacent garden.

Electronics and Lack of Servants Influence Design

Most American homes are now maidless so that kitchen and dining habits are being subjected to change. The house that is without benefit of maid or laundress, naturally becomes a haven for every possible labor-saving and automatic device. This lack of permanent help has brought on a hey-day of gadgetry.

An intimate quality is lent to areas for conversation and dining by screens and lighting effects. The bubble lamp (reflected in glass wall above) casts a direct down spotlight on the table, as well as a general glow. The extension of the brick terrace and bedroom walls adds a considerable sense of space to the small dining area. A breakfast counter, with pass through to kitchen, doubles as a serving buffet.

The interest added to all interiors by the undulating roof can be clearly noted in the photo at far left. Center skylight can be seen above the screen.

"External form should be the interpreter of internal purpose."   R. D. OWEN, 1848

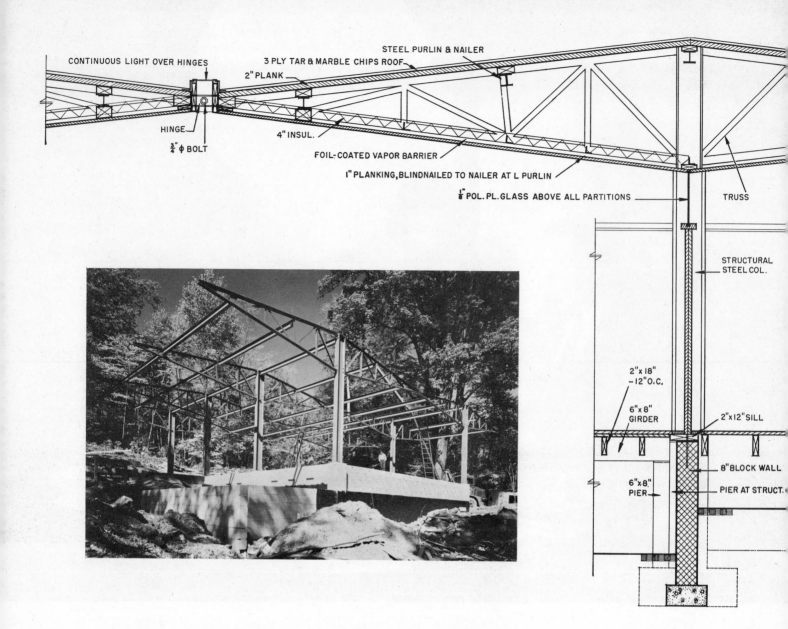

CONTINUOUS LIGHT OVER HINGES

3 PLY TAR & MARBLE CHIPS ROOF

STEEL PURLIN & NAILER

2" PLANK

HINGE

$\frac{3}{4}" \phi$ BOLT

4" INSUL.

FOIL-COATED VAPOR BARRIER

I" PLANKING, BLINDNAILED TO NAILER AT L PURLIN

$\frac{1}{8}"$ POL. PL. GLASS ABOVE ALL PARTITIONS

TRUSS

STRUCTURAL STEEL COL.

2" x 18" —12" O.C.

6" x 8" GIRDER

2" x 12" SILL

6" x 8" PIER

8" BLOCK WALL

PIER AT STRUCT.

"Electronics," if that is the word, are making over our living space, and remolding our daily home life. In the house that we occupy today, we are rather sure to find television, radio, a Hi-Fi record player, a tape recorder, film projector, a device to waken us in the morning and to sing us to sleep at night, plus a variety of automatic controls for opening ventilators and controlling temperature. Lewis Mumford, in pondering over these aids to living, seems to intimate that a time might arrive when, as in Butler's *Erewhon*, mechanical invention will become a crime and machines will be assigned to the museum as a warning to the human race! At the same time, these have certainly brought more comfort and convenience to the American house.

The nature of this suburban house and its plan provisions is shaped directly by family habits and activities: hobbies, entertaining of friends around the terrace grill, weekend parties, Cub Scout meetings, and gardening. Other plan features have sprung from principles of child welfare, such as a combined library and mechanical work room varied with the advancement of the child. The trend of including both a family room and a separate living room also reflect this thinking.

Outdoor life, along with the desire for sunshine and recreation, is also contributing to the reshaping of the house, giving us game rooms and

The unique structure of the Franzen house resulted in a number of savings. The very light steel sections actually form a three-hinged arch. The diamond frames are mostly 2 by 2 by ¼ inch angles, welded, and permitted easy handling and fabrication. All structural members were erected in one day. The free-standing, water-tight roof permitted all trades to work on the building simultaneously and without interruption by inclement weather. It also eliminated load bearing walls and partitions. Interior finishes are warm colored, very durable — as in playroom, left.

"*Cannot our Architects furnish us with a truly American style? Will not something original in time be produced?*"

L. C. TUTHILL, 1848

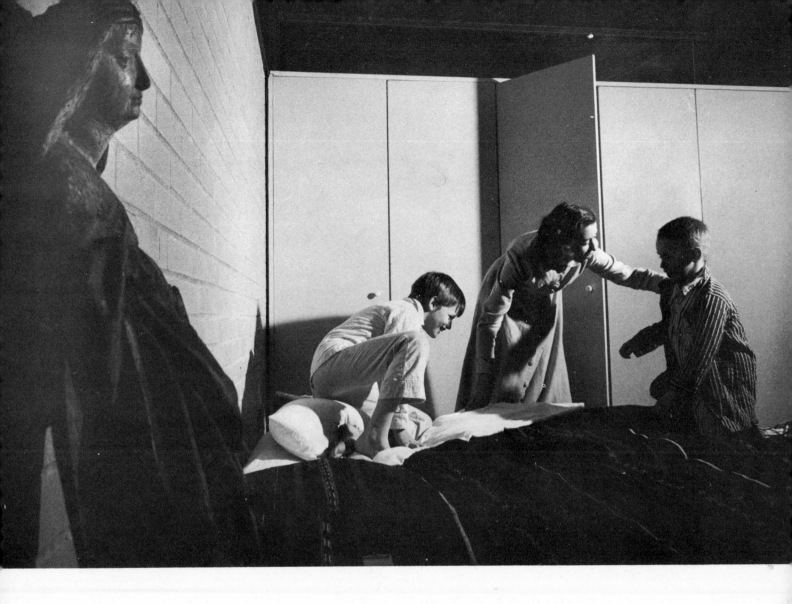

terraces for leisurely sitting and sunbathing. The basement playroom has often been brought up to the first floor because its former location was inconvenient, and difficult for the mother's supervision of young children. The same is the case with the heater room and laundry. These are dignified by a ground level position, sometimes placed as an adjunct of the kitchen, and, at the same time, convenient to a service yard, screened by shrubbery from the garden terrace. A workshop may become an annex to the garage or carport. The do-it-yourself fad has given us a first-aid-bar as a replacement for our first-aid-kit!

There is a familiar vocabulary associated with modern design indicative of a changing manner of building. Some of the descriptive terms are: fluidity of space, rational structural system, cantilever support, prefabricated units, modular panels, shed, undulating, and butterfly roofs. The "picture window" is becoming an almost obsolete term, in the wake of the side-sliding, ball-bearing, floor to ceiling sash. The wide projecting eaves, to shield the house from intense southern sun, have practical meaning for the air conditioned home. Floor surfaces have been improved by the introduction of materials that retain their gloss, even with hard usage, and that require little or no polishing. Houses placed on a site with a gentle slope are sometimes designed with what is termed a

Privacy and quiet are well established in the bedrooms, in spite of the apparent openness. Glass panels fill the areas above partitions and storage walls, and reduce noise amazingly well.

In spite of its small actual size, the Franzen house provides an enormous amount of living area, including four bedrooms (one bedroom doubles as the playroom). Rooms are quite small, but simple furnishings and finishes, and the close visual connection with the outdoors make them seem very large.

"Iron and glass requires an entirely different style from that which sprung from the rocks of Egypt, and the masses of marble with which the lintels of the Grecian temples were formed."
WRITINGS OF JOSEPH HENRY, 1856

"split-level," which, like split-personalities, may have their own peculiar attraction.

It is not unusual today to have rooms with controlled openings to the sky, at the center of the house. Screens to windows can now be raised or lowered by push button control. Experiments are being made to improve the use of screening; some have even proposed abolishing all screening by the substitution of periodical applications of insect repelling spray around the house and at all windows and doors. This is now being applied at the Franzen house. Increased interior daylight has encouraged the planting of shrubs indoors. This is favored, not alone for appearance, but also to contribute to the maintenance of a healthful humidity level.

If we were to summarize the more noticeable and hopeful tendencies in domestic design by architects of the past years, recognition would be made of the gradual acceptance of new building processes and factory produced materials. Herein lies a new esthetic and an indigenous quality. There is also a promise of adding enrichment and authenticity to our national architecture. While originality was the least of the virtues that the architect of the nineteenth century wished to possess, it becomes the aim and the goal of his twentieth century successor.

EAST

THE ARCHITECTS COLLABORATIVE, ARCHITECTS. *Mr. and Mrs. David Pickman, Owners. Location: Bedford, Massachusetts. Stanley I. Phalen, Contractor.*

LOUIS REENS

GLAZED STAIRWELL LENDS DRAMA

The simple massing and exterior treatment of this white-painted house is sparked with considerable drama by a glassed-in, two story stair hall that serves as entry and connecting link for the two wings of the house. The plan is designed to separate various family activities, and the design is deliberately understated to focus attention on its site.

The house sits on about 13 acres of wooded land overlooking the Concord River in "Thoreau Country." The large impressive trees were planted by the owners' grandfather and have been cared for each season. The owners wanted the house to be secondary to all this; the exterior was thus designed in quiet, clean planes, with the exterior of redwood, cedar clapboards and brick chimney — all painted the same color.

Interior spaces are extended into the open by a flagstone dining porch and a bluestone terrace. A sunken play court in the back (photo above) provides daylight and an access to the outdoors for the basement playroom.

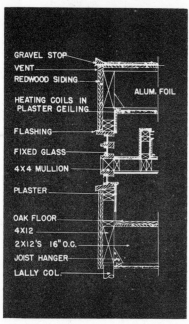

GRAVEL STOP
VENT
REDWOOD SIDING
ALUM. FOIL
HEATING COILS IN
PLASTER CEILING
FLASHING
FIXED GLASS
4X4 MULLION
PLASTER
OAK FLOOR
4X12
2X12'S 16" O.C.
JOIST HANGER
LALLY COL.

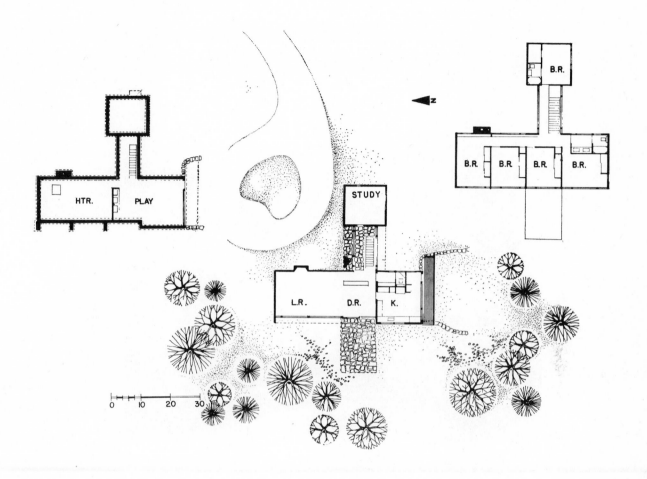

Mr. and Mrs. Pickman requested that the master bedroom and bath have some degree of separation from the children's bedrooms. This was accomplished by placing the master bedroom over the study with its access across a kind of link bridge in the glazed stair hall. A further separation of noisy and quiet activities was accomplished by placing the playroom on the basement level.

A small area off the kitchen serves as a "mudroom" for the children to take off boots and snowsuits. The interiors (see living room, left) combine traditional furniture with the modern house.

PATIO SPLITS TWO-ZONE HOUSE

The dramatic two-zone plan of this house separates formal and informal living areas by means of a central courtyard flanked on both sides by parallel wings. A rugged stone wall merges artfully with the heavily wooded landscape which surrounds the house, and yet is a forceful enough barrier to yield a secure sense of well-defined containment.

The bedroom area and living area are in separate wings. Covered walks at either end of the courtyard connect them. Entrance to either must be gained by traveling outside, along the walks. Walks could be glass-enclosed, though the sun and the heat which radiates from the house keep them free of snow — even during Connecticut winters.

The stone wall which closes in the garden (and house) at opposite ends is divided by massive wood doors which slide open to create dual gates to the garden (photo right). Closed, the doors offer protection against storms. The garden, which in effect becomes a room in the house, is well cultivated to contrast with rough surrounding landscape.

ELIOT NOYES, ARCHITECT *and Owner. Location: New Canaan, Connecticut. Borglum and Meek, Inc., Contractor.*
Richard Kelly, Lighting Consultant

1957 First Honor Award, National AIA Award Program;
1957 First Honor Award, AIA, House & Home, Better Homes & Gardens, and NBC Award Program;
1957 Award of Merit, House & Home, in recognition of outstanding contribution to housing progress;
1957 Award of Merit, Centennial Committee of New England Regional Council AIA

© EZRA STOLLER

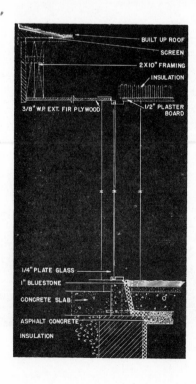

BUILT UP ROOF

SCREEN

2 X 10" FRAMING

INSULATION

3/8" W.P. EXT. FIR PLYWOOD

1/2" PLASTER BOARD

1/4" PLATE GLASS

1" BLUESTONE

CONCRETE SLAB

ASPHALT CONCRETE

INSULATION

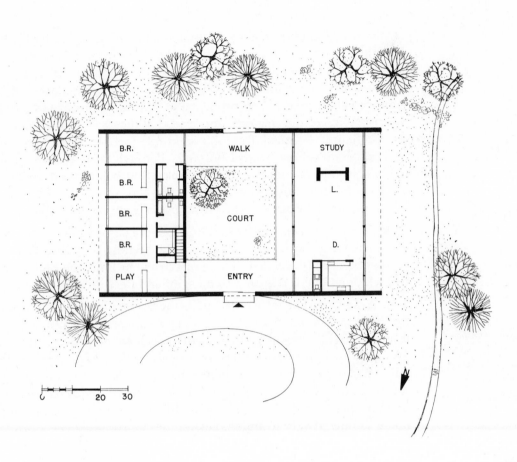

Plan of the Eliot Noyes house puts five bedrooms, baths, snackbar, laundry, storage, and sitting room areas along one wing. Four of the bedrooms face the Connecticut woods. The master bedroom spans the width of the wing, yielding a view of both woods and court-yard. The sitting room (photo page 31) doubles as a playroom for the children and a family T.V. room. A snack bar equipped with combination refrigerator and range serves for early morning coffee and late evening snacks. The other wing is composed of kitchen, dining area, living room and study. The kitchen is a compact horseshoe shape with pass-through to dining area. Living and dining areas are together, separated only by placement of furniture (photo top left). Focal point in the living room is a stone-and-plaster fireplace which screens study. Floors are bluestone, walls are glass. Study (photo bottom left) is furnished with long table, bookshelves. Skylights in the study, which doubles as working area or extension of living room, provide additional natural lighting.

HOUSE DESIGNED FOR A WAY OF LIFE

A FAMILY'S PATTERN of living is usually set in great degree by the house they live in, by the facilities and background it provides for activities. All contemporary architecture is generally associated with informal, servantless daily life. But there are many who, faced with the same economic and labor problems as the ultra-modernists, wish to preserve some of the elegance and tradition they have grown up with.

This house, designed by John Pekruhn for Mr. and Mrs. R. D. McGranahan, in Fox Chapel Borough, Pennsylvania, astutely balances the two schools of thought. It is completely unstereotyped, efficient — and provides for family casualness, company formality. Interior and exterior echo this balance, with fresh use of familiar materials.

THE NEIGHBORHOOD: Fox Chapel Borough is a conservative, fashionable, north-eastern suburb of Pittsburgh. The terrain is rolling to rugged, with parts heavily wooded. There are stringent limits on plot sizes and setbacks, and one is required to have an architect to build there.

THE SITE: the architect worked with the owners in choosing a plot for the house. A wooded area was a major interest. After looking at a number of sites together, they finally decided on the location used. Strangely enough it was a piece of property which Mrs. McGranahan's father had owned for years. It hadn't been built upon because of a great ravine in the middle, which, with the setback requirements, made ordinary placement of a house fairly difficult. But for a non-traditional house, it offered very dramatic possibilities.

John Pekruhn, Architect. Garrett-Murrell, Inc., Contractor.

A sweeping, cantilevered deck dominates the McGranahan house, adding living space to the upper level, sheltering bedrooms below. Exterior is brick and wood, painted soft red and white

JOSEPH W. MOLITOR

THE FAMILY: the McGranahans have "a houseful of young children", and wanted a house for family living, yet at the same time easily adaptable for formal and informal entertaining without interfering with the regular routine of the children. For large parties and dinners, they have local caterers bring in much of the food already prepared.

THE HOUSE: the plan is organized with living areas on the main level, sleeping quarters below. Two living rooms are provided, family and formal, which enables one part of the house to be messed up while the other remains serene for sudden company. The kitchen is actually part of the family room, and functions as a control center from which the dining room, family room, deck and children's play area can be surveyed or served. The small, efficient area of the kitchen is expanded by family room space when the caterers move in. At such times, the childrens' meals are served here at a counter.

The laundry is placed on the bedroom level to simplify the chore of carrying clothes and linen to and from bedrooms and baths. An exhaust fan eliminates laundry odors.

THE ARCHITECT: John Pekruhn states that, "basically, I think the McGranahans wanted a house that was very efficient, as regards operation, yet at the same time very dramatic. With the dramatic site to work with, the latter wasn't too difficult to accomplish — we just put the deck flying out into the tree tops. Mrs. McGranahan's clever ideas in regard to the operation of the house brought off the former."

OWNERS' REACTION: "Our house is extremely satisfying to live in. Pitched ceilings and glass walls somehow produce two opposite effects — snugness, spaciousness. We're full of praise for kitchen and laundry."

The front of the house has some of the simple formality of the living room (left). In plan note the use of a generous driveway, entrance terrace, the roofed section linking garage to house. Family room (below and right) features durable, easy to keep surfaces and furnishings

JOSEPH W. MOLITOR

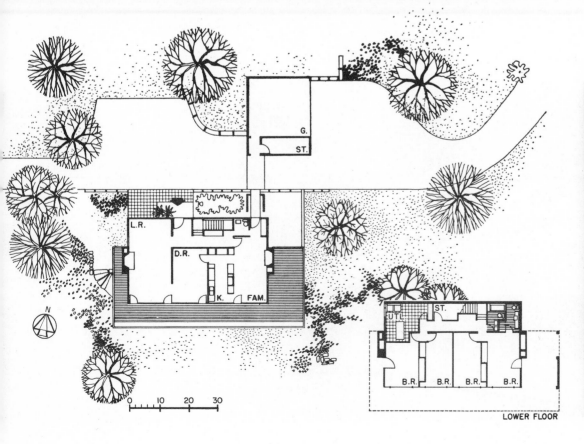

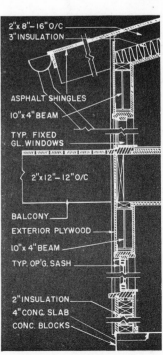

2"x 8"—16" O/C
3" INSULATION

ASPHALT SHINGLES
10"x 4" BEAM

TYP. FIXED
GL. WINDOWS

2"x 12"—12" O/C

BALCONY
EXTERIOR PLYWOOD
10"x 4" BEAM
TYP. OP'G. SASH

2" INSULATION
4" CONC. SLAB
CONC. BLOCKS

G.
ST.

L.R.

D.R.

C

K. FAM.

N

0   10   20   30

UTL   ST.

B.R.   B.R.   B.R.   B.R.

LOWER FLOOR

Space outside the McGranahan house is organized into areas of varying use: living deck, dining terrace, service area with children's playground, quiet areas off the bedrooms. Lights below deck shine on trees around house at night

CHARD F. WEBB, ARCHITECT AND OWNER.
Locaton: Phoenixville, Pennsylvania
Irvin Smerly, Contractor.

COMPACT DELIGHT

Compactness is an element necessary in the design of any fine small home. When it is executed logically and with finesse, as in the design of this house, compactness may also yield a dramatic sense of order and completion. A living room, kitchen and dining room, two children's bedrooms, playroom, two bathrooms, master suite, and an unusually large concentration of storage space have been fitted neatly and without cramping into a 34-ft -sq. structure.

Rather than leveling the grade of an already existing slope on the site, the house was raised 8 ft above the lowest ground point. This created space for a carport under the living area and kept the commonly sub-surface storage and utility room at ground level. The structural frame, composed of 8- by 12-in. steel beams, is supported by nine 3- by 6-in. steel tubes which are secured in 3- by 3-ft concrete footings. An 8-in. concrete wall forms the foundation.

Stairwell, Fireplace Liven Limited Space . . .

A cage of 2- by 6-in. vertical fir studs around the stairwell extends from ground floor level to the roof. The cage gives a sense of enclosure to the stairwell without disturbing the flow of space in the living area (left). The vertical stud pattern is repeated in an exterior fin (see photo, page previous) which keeps the otherwise square house from looking "boxy."

Entrance to the house is made directly from the carport. Floor-to-ceiling glass panels allow a view to dramatic stairwell (photo below). Laundry, storage, and mechanical rooms are beyond.

A stone wall, on which the house seems to rest (see exterior photo, previous page), penetrates the floor and extends into the living area to become the foundation for the fireplace (bottom).

BEN SCHNALL

Plate I

WEBB

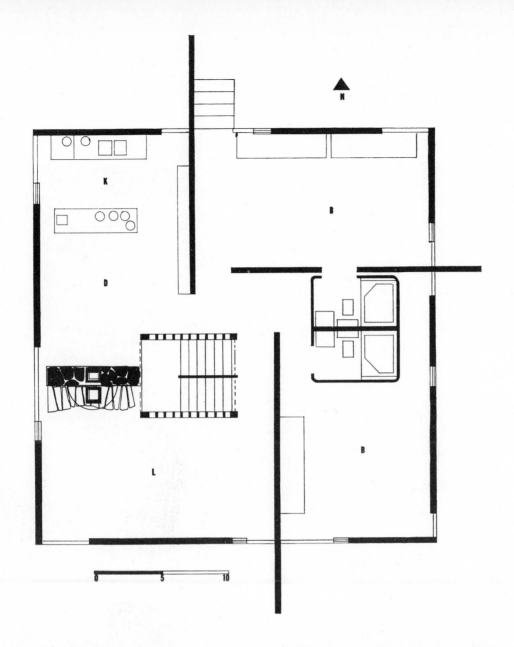

The warm color and grain of the exposed vertical studs contrast nicely with the white plaster walls and fireplace in the living area. The bell-shaped hood and flue of the fireplace are asbestos coated and covered with ¾-in.-thick low soluble cement which was troweled smooth.

Built-ins Divide Rooms, Multiply Space . . .

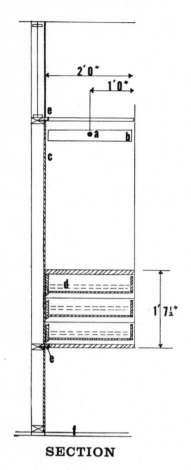

SECTION

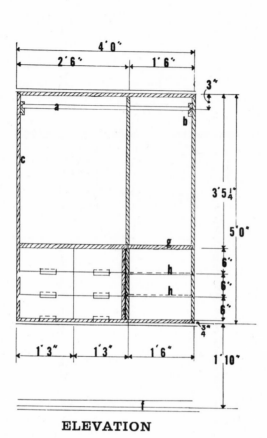

ELEVATION

LEGEND FOR SECTIONS AND ELE-VATION: a. 1-in. steel pipe; b. ¾-in. by 3-in. side cleat; c. ¼-in. birch plywood panel; d. ¾-in. hardwood guides; e. fastener; f. floor; g. ¾-in. removable plywood shelf; h. ½-in. plywood shelf; i. ¾-in. plywood sliding doors on sash balance; j. 12-gauge copper hood and exhaust; k. ¼-in. white Georgian marble top, cut out for griddle and burners; l. converter outlet; m. two-way sliding drawers.

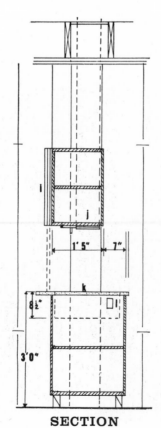

SECTION

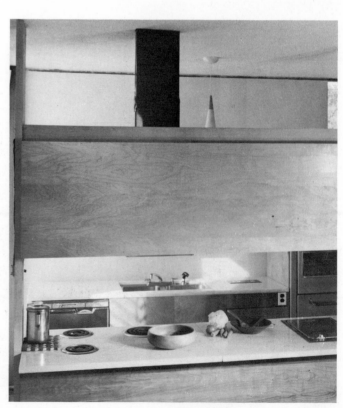

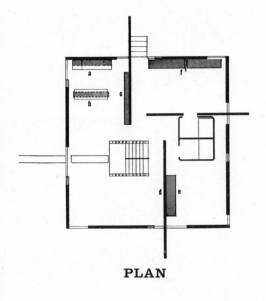

PLAN

Built-in storage and wardrobe units, space-saving devices in themselves, have been put to a second use as room partitions in this extremely compact house. The section, elevation, and photo at left show how boxes of lumbercore birch plywood have been hung from vertical studs and fitted with rods and adjustable shelves to form wardrobe units which serve also as partitions (see e and f on plan). To make the units as convenient as possible for storing clothes, the family was measured for sizes, and amounts of clothing were approximated. Each member was then given one basic unit with heights of rod and shelves adjusted to his or her particular need. The total height of each unit corresponds with the height of all other partitions and built-ins in the house. Enough space was left below each unit to fit beds, facilitate cleaning, or store books and toys. Bamboo matchstick curtains hung on a brass rod cover the units instead of space-taking conventional doors.

Kitchen equipment is built into two parallel counter and cabinet units (see a and b on plan). The photo at bottom left looks through the griddle and range counter unit to the sink and oven counter. A plywood panel (see section next to photo) slides down to close the pass-through from range and griddle counter to dining area. A china cabinet is hung from the wall dividing the children's bedroom and the kitchen (see c on plan). Drawers in storage walls (see photos and section below) open from either side.

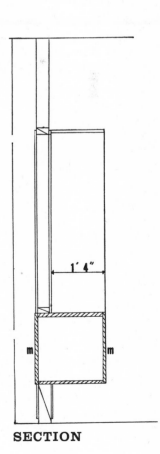

SECTION

DISCIPLINED ROMANTICISM

This idyllic house blends two strong, yet often quite divergent trends: a rational, regulated neo-Palladian influence dominates the plan and balanced design; a decided romantic turn is obvious in the setting, bridge-like construction, vaulted roof, terracotta-colored stucco exterior (patterned with bas reliefs)—and gargoyles for downspouts. The central, glassed-in living pavilion is flanked by four masonry square wings, one at each corner. These wings zone the house for its various functions. One provides for servant's room, kitchen and laundry. Another has three family bedrooms and a bath. A third has the master bedroom, dressing room and bath. The fourth contains a study-guest room, powder room, and a quiet, walled-in court. The wings have flat roofs and 9 ft high ceilings, while the dominant central "living bridge" has three arches rising 13 ft from the floor. Finishes throughout are rich in tone: gold leaf on the vaulted ceiling, terrazzo floors, ebonized wood cabinets.

ROBERT DAMORA, *Courtesy of* HOUSE & GARDEN

JOHN MacL. JOHANSEN, ARCHITECT.
Location: Connecticut.
Richard Kelly, Light Consultant.
Wenzel Co. Inc., Contractors.
James Fanning, Landscape Architect.

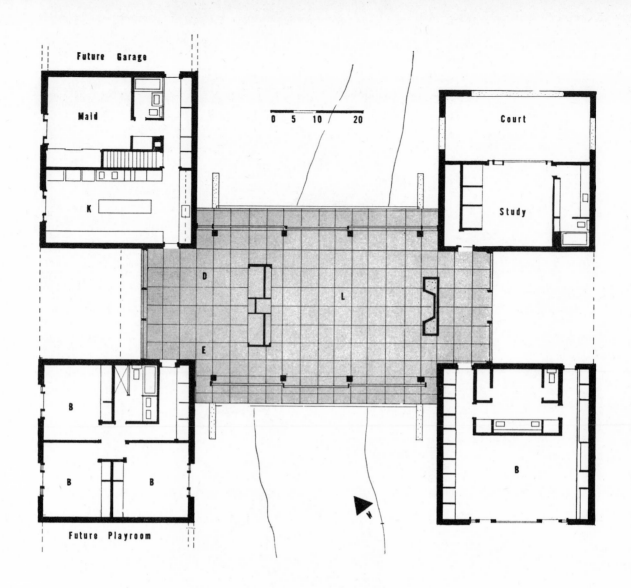

House In Connecticut: A Blend Of Comfort And Formality . . .

The four wings of the house offer quiet retreats, privacy from the open general living areas.

The master bedroom suite is ranged with built-in storage units, reducing furniture requirements to a minimum (photo far left).

The living room (above) is wide open to views up and down stream to pools and falls, terraces, another bridge, and very fine oak trees. Balconies run along either side, with access through four doors, sliding glass (left center).

The kitchen (near left) is unusually commodious, with multiple units of most of the standard fixtures. A breakfast nook is at the far end. Kitchen and all interior baths have skylights.

JOHANSEN | 47

ROBERT DAMORA, *Courtesy of* HOUSE & GARDEN

Above: the glass-walled living room bridge creates a highly pleasant, resort-like atmosphere.

Top right: plan for the steel and concrete bridge construction.

Right: cross section through center of bridge.

Below: longitudinal section through house, showing entrance, living and dining areas, passage.

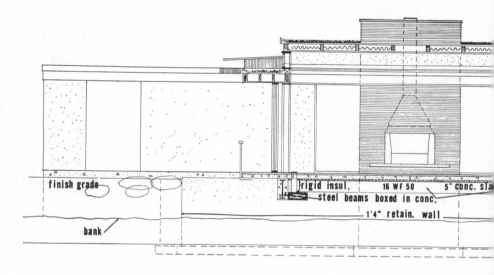

finish grade

rigid insul.   16 WF 50   5" conc. sla

steel beams boxed in conc.

1'4" retain. wall

bank

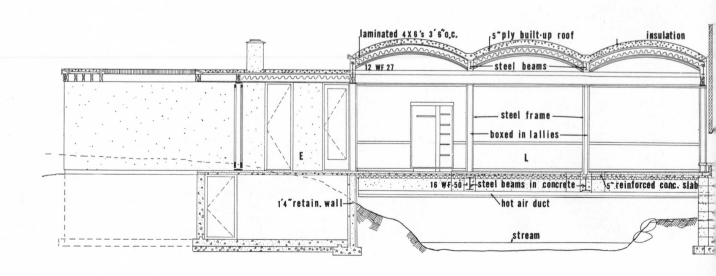

laminated 4 X 6's 3' 6" O.C.   5" ply built-up roof   insulation

12 WF 27   steel beams

steel frame

boxed in lallies

E   L

16 WF 50   steel beams in concrete   5" reinforced conc. slab

1'4" retain. wall   hot air duct

stream

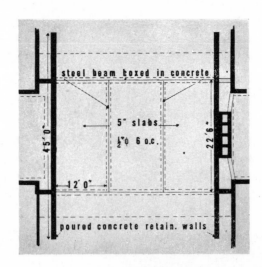

House in Connecticut:
A Rippling-Roofed Bridge Forms A Romantic Living Area . . .

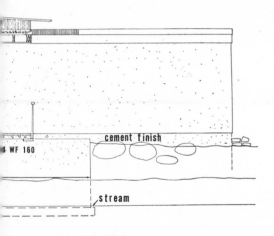

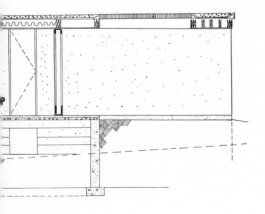

Although this house would be effective in any setting, the one in which it is placed (see photo pages 44-45) dramatizes the central living pavilion. This unit is built as a simple steel and concrete bridge over the quiet, shallow stream which meanders through the property. The wings and retaining walls anchor it firmly, visually and in reality, to the banks of the stream. Sliding glass doors, which link it with balconies at either side, permit the entire bridge to be used as a sheltered, open-air terrace in fine summer weather. Doors are aluminum.

The bridge contains dining and living areas, separated by a bar and hi-fi cabinet. This space is extended at either end by front and rear entrance halls. Floors (including balconies) are gray-black terrazzo. Insulated, galvanized sheet metal ducts run beneath the bridge for forced hot air heating. The basement and retaining walls are reinforced concrete; concrete block is used for crawl spaces and to frame the rest of the house. The exterior walls are finished with integral color stucco. The fireplace and chimney are glazed brick. The vaulted roof has a gold leaf paper ceiling, aluminum accordion insulation, copper flashing. Gargoyles by sculptor Robert Engman serve as downspouts over the stream.

SHERWOOD, MILLS AND SMITH, ARCHITECTS. *Mr. and Mrs. Willis N. Mills, Owners. Location: New Canaan, Connecticut. Barglum and Meek, Builders.*

BALCONIES ADD CHARM AND SPACE

The generous use of balconies and terraces in the design of this hillside house lends charm and spaciousness to an already distinctive plan. Working with a particularly difficult site problem, the architects have produced an effective and dramatic solution by designing this two-story house to rest midway down a steep, rocky slope.

The site is composed of two fairly level areas separated by rocky cliffs and tall trees. Differences in elevation of the two levels is about 45 ft. The architects decided to build the house on the slope to take advantage of the view and the natural, rugged background. The plan situates the living area about midway on the slope, with the bedroom and entrance level above. An outdoor terrace, bordered with planters, extends from the living area level. The living room itself rises to the full height of the house. The rest of the structure is divided into two stories. A balcony projects out from the second-story floor level, providing an overhang which shades a portion of the terrace below.

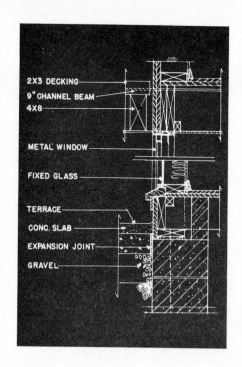

2X3 DECKING
9" CHANNEL BEAM
4X8

METAL WINDOW

FIXED GLASS

TERRACE
CONC. SLAB
EXPANSION JOINT
GRAVEL

JOSEPH W. MOLITOR

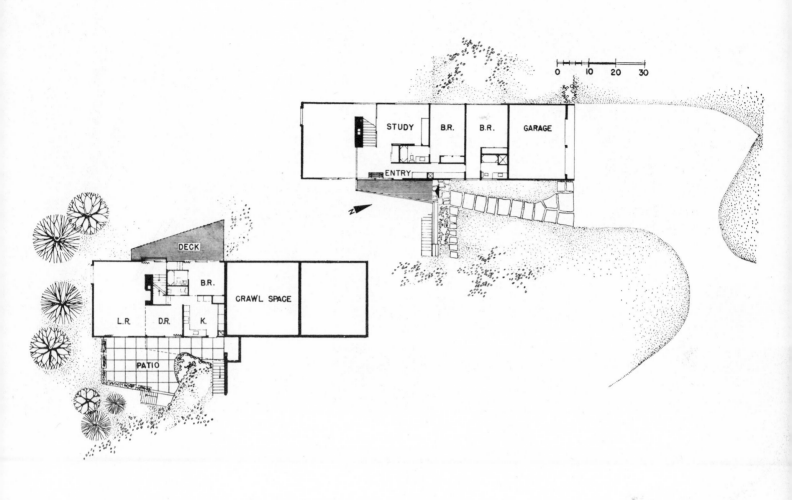

STUDY B.R. B.R. GARAGE

ENTRY

0 10 20 30

DECK

B.R.

CRAWL SPACE

L.R. D.R. K.

PATIO

A sun deck on the west side of the Mills house is sheltered from the north by a natural rock ledge. Below the main front terrace is another covered terrace. A gentle slope leads to the meadow below. The entrance lobby looks down into the two-story living room. Warm interior colors were selected by the owner-architect's wife to blend with the natural colors of the site. A light cerulean blue ceiling, which continues from the living room through the study and entrance hall, offers color contrast and accentuates flow of space. Exterior finish is natural redwood vertical siding with white trim.

A PAVILION FOR LIVING

The zoning of interior spaces is clearly and dramatically expressed in this precisely balanced house. Private rooms (bedrooms, study, baths, services) are housed in the low, closed, brick-veneered wings. Windows are at the sides. Living areas, by contrast, open wide to the outside beneath a tall soaring roof supported by four steel columns. The space is further expanded, front and back (see photos) by wide terraces. Glass all around emphasizes the roof's lightness, takes full advantage of the wooded, relatively secluded site. Low partitions inside also accent the great sense of space. The foundations of the house are concrete slab on grade; the frame is welded steel, with a 4-in. brick veneer exterior. The roof is built-up, with a ceiling of 6-in. fir boarding on the underside. Copings, scuppers and sliding doors are aluminum; screens are bronze. Heating is by a warm air perimeter system.

ULRICH FRANZEN, ARCHITECT.
Mr. and Mrs. Richard Beattie, Owners.
Location: Rye, New York.
August Nelson, Contractor.

1959 Award of Merit, National AIA Award Program

In the living area (above), a depressed pit in front of fireplace adds space by keeping major seating low, eliminates massive sofa frames. Wall-hung storage cabinets, with lights at bottom and top, further minimize furniture requirements. Floors are laminated walnut blocks; walls are plasterboard.

The entrance hall (right) gives visual sweep across entire 30-by 30-ft pavilion. Ceiling is 10½ ft high. Birch cabinets and a screen wall block view of dining and sitting areas.

Rooms in the two wings are small, but comfortably adequate. They are made to appear proportionately larger by using low (7½-ft) ceilings, keeping decor simple. The study (right center) can double as a guest bedroom. The furnace room is beneath it, accessible through a trap door in the floor.

Planned spatial effects also add size to the master bathroom (far right): neat commodious built-ins, a wall of mirrors, a plastic dome ceiling over the tub compartment. Walls and ceiling are glazed tile, floors are unglazed tile.

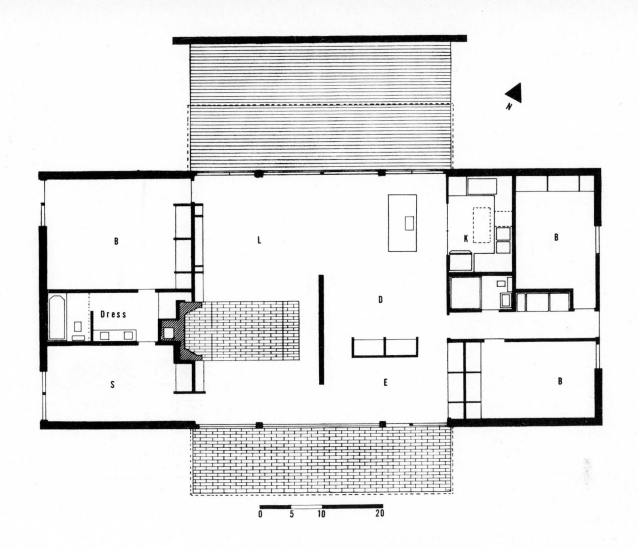

B

L

K

B

Dress

D

S

E

B

0   5   10   20

Visual Effects Add Spaciousness . . .

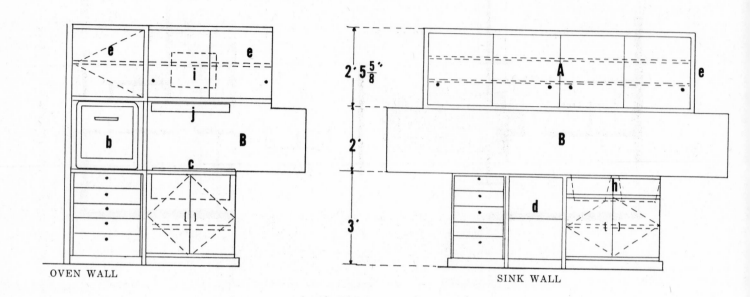

OVEN WALL

SINK WALL

The Kitchen is "Cafeteria-Style" . . .

Easy to cook in; easy to serve from; easy to maintain: these three prime requirements for a small house kitchen are well met here. This space-saving, but fully equipped kitchen also offers an interestingly different plan arrangement. The cooking area is a convenient, and more-or-less standardized U shape, with work centers and counters nicely grouped. The addition of a convertible bar-breakfast-serving-counter as a free-standing unit in the living area adds considerable, and practical, flexibility to the arrangement.

For everyday, family living, double doors open the kitchen wide to the living area, and the counter can be used directly as a breakfast or snack counter. On other occasions it is designed to be used as a "cafeteria-style" buffet, with informal service from the kitchen side, the "cafeteria-line" on the other. For more formal entertaining, the kitchen is closed off, and the front of the counter unit is closed to become a serving counter with food out of sight. For cocktail parties, a sink with a removable lid converts it to a bar. The kitchen has vinyl tile floors, and is lighted by fluorescent tubes under the cabinets and a plastic dome skylight.

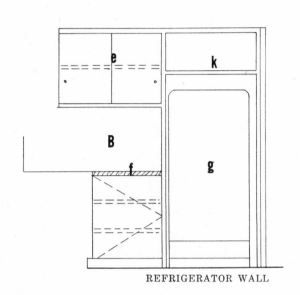

REFRIGERATOR WALL

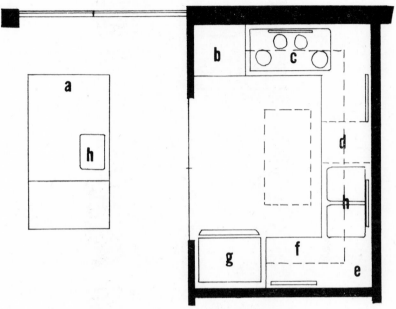

PLAN OF BAR COUNTER AND KITCHEN

© EZRA STOLLER

© EZRA STOLLER

EASE AND ORDER IN THE SUBURBS

This highly stylized, elegant little house is an excellent example of the school of thought that concentrates on order, balance, and perfection of workmanship. It is also a very livable house for a family that leans toward neatness and formality — which many do.

The bold overall concept of the house — the simplest rectangular shape, perfectly symmetrical façades — is softened by a number of subtle touches. The most important of these is, perhaps, the careful integration of the house with its site. Trees, terraces, garden walls, walks, all become integral parts of the design. These means are also used everywhere for planned extended vistas, as can be noted in the photos above. Quiet contrasts of materials play a big part, too. Painted facias are contrasted with the pattern of brick, the sleekness of glass; smooth flagstone floors abut polished wood walls.

The formal alternation of glazed and solid wall sections works well with the plan, giving both areas of privacy and views to each room in the house.

PHILIP JOHNSON, ARCHITECT. *Dr. and Mrs. J. E. Miller, Owners. Location: Irvington-on-Hudson, New York.*

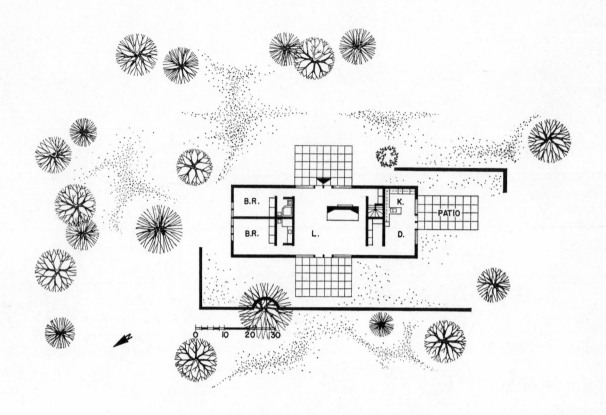

Facilities are abundant in the J. E. Miller house for indoor-outdoor living. There is a terrace off each room. The area off the sparkling white dining kitchen (left) serves as a dining patio, screened from the street by a brick wall. From the front, this wall enormously increases the apparent size of the house and offsets its absolute symmetry.

At the back, a low brick retaining wall defines a large living terrace overlooking the Hudson river. The part of the terrace immediately adjoining the living area is paved, the rest is a neat lawn (see photo right of living area).

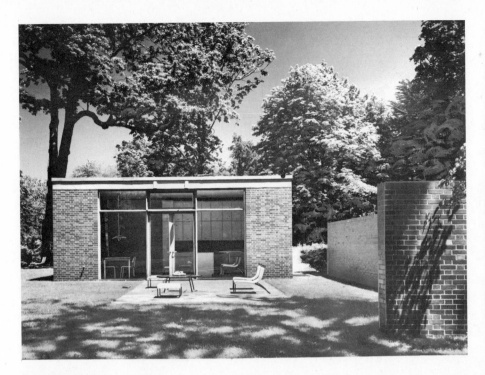

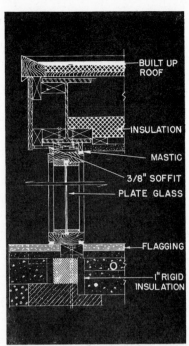

BUILT UP ROOF

INSULATION

MASTIC

3/8" SOFFIT

PLATE GLASS

FLAGGING

1" RIGID INSULATION

DAVIS, BRODY, JUSTER AND WISNIEWSKI, ARCHITECTS. (*Now* DAVIS, BRODY AND WISNIEWSKI).
Mr. and Mrs. Gustave E. Rosenau, Owners. Location: Huntington Valley, Pennsylvania.
Adams Construction Co., Contractors. Wiesenfeld and Hayward,
Structural Engineers. Fred Blau, Landscape Architect

CONVERTIBLE PLAN PROVIDES SPACE

Visiting children and their offspring can pose a major planning problem in a house for an older couple. Frequently, the resulting home seems too big for comfort and easy maintenance when the couple are there alone. Or, if it is planned just for the parents — it can be much too small when the children arrive. By the use of highly flexible, multi-use living areas, this modest but extremely pleasant house adapts quickly to either situation. Spacious daytime areas for family gatherings can be divided into several sleeping rooms for those that stay overnight.

The living areas include spaces for sitting, dining, music, games, studio (the wife is a painter), and display gallery. Divisions are suggested by head-height bookcases, cabinets, screens, and a unique round bathroom. Screens and curtains close to create three distinct rooms, each with access from the gallery. The master bedroom is a quiet area at one end of the house, a servant's or children's suite is at the other.

The house is designed to fit quietly and unobtrusively on its site — the edge of a beautifully wooded bluff. From the front, the house is shielded by an arrangement of baffle fences. One steps down from the drive into a delightful, and surprising, Japanese court (above). The glass-walled gallery looks out upon it, but Shoji screens (detail, right) give privacy. From this point, carefully planned vistas are encountered throughout the house. At the back, windows and sliding doors link living areas with the terrace and emphasize the view (above left).

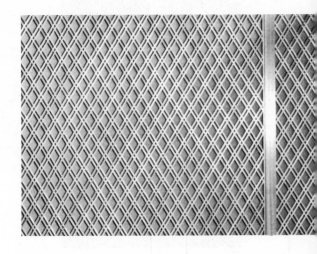

MARC NEUHOF

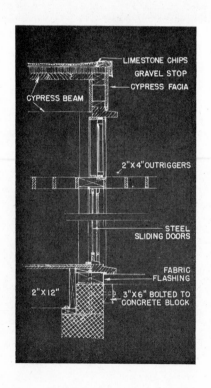

LIMESTONE CHIPS
GRAVEL STOP
CYPRESS FACIA

CYPRESS BEAM

2"X 4" OUTRIGGERS

STEEL
SLIDING DOORS

FABRIC
FLASHING

2"X 12"   3"X 6" BOLTED TO
CONCRETE BLOCK

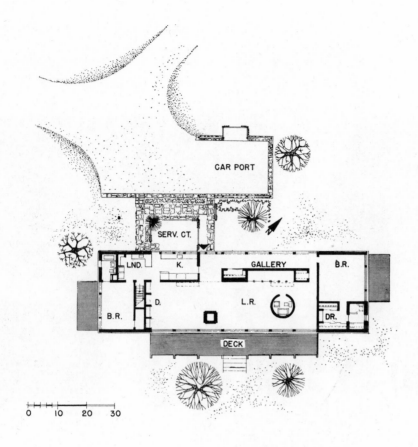

CAR PORT

SERV. CT.

LND. K. GALLERY B.R.

D. L.R. DR.

B.R.

DECK

0 10 20 30

Along with the vistas planned for each room in the Rosenau house, thoughtful attention has been given to the quality and control of light — inside and out, daytime and night. Downlights edge the roof to light gardens and terraces, add a party sparkle (note in photos on preceding page). Glass walls admit light on gray days, but sunlight is tempered by pierced screens, curtains and louvered overhangs. Skylights provide natural or artificial illumination to light up interior walls. In the display gallery, a ceiling channel permits spotlights to be placed wherever desired.

A COUNTRY HOUSE ON A PLATFORM

A fresh, new use of a raised terrace, coupled with a sensitively designed open plan, marks this as a very distinguished house for a small family. The deft blend of casualness and formality in its design also makes it unusually adaptable, for its size, to the inevitable variety of everyday and special family activities.

Although the idea of raising a house on a "platform" is hardly new (it has been associated with buildings in the Grand Manner, of course, all through history), the freshness lies in its use to such advantage for a small house. On a country hilltop site as this, it gives the house importance and expands the defined living area. It also minimizes the maintenance of sizeable grounds. Garden areas and lawns are confined to platform. The rest of the land needs only rough, occasional mowing. The entrance garden (photo right) is planned to look well winter and summer: myrtle and ivy are used as ground cover, with flowers peeking through in season.

EDWARD LARRABEE BARNES, ARCHITECT *and Owner. Location: Mount Kisco, New York. August Nelson,* *Contractor. James Fanning, Landscape Architect. Benjamin Spivak, Heating Engineer*

BEN SCHNALL

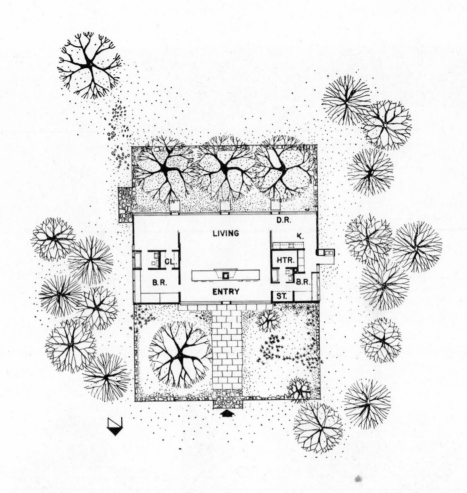

The plan of the Edward Barnes house is basically conceived as one big room which combines terrace, living area, entrance hall, master bedroom and kitchen. Yet each individual area has its own importance and privacy. The bedroom doubles as a library, with the bed set back from living room view. A sliding door can close off the room.

The kitchen is treated as a major room, with full windows and careful detailing. It includes a pleasant dining area. The food preparation area is screened from the living room, and there is a sliding door. The dining table is moved to the living room for large parties. A convenient service entrance adjoins the kitchen and contains the laundry.

The main entrance hall is defined by a storage wall flanking the fireplace. The cabinets are fitted to store outdoor clothes, tools, linen, hi-fi equipment and games. As in the rest of the house, storage is well planned and handled in a neat, unobtrusive manner. The entire back wall of the house is of glass, shielded by trees and outside blinds.

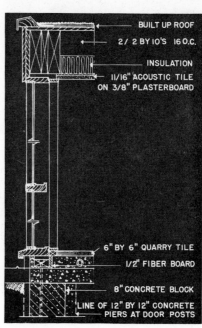

BUILT UP ROOF

2/ 2 BY IO'S I6 O.C.

INSULATION

II/I6" ACOUSTIC TILE
ON 3/8" PLASTERBOARD

6" BY 6" QUARRY TILE

I/2" FIBER BOARD

8" CONCRETE BLOCK

LINE OF I2" BY I2" CONCRETE
PIERS AT DOOR POSTS

TEXTURE SPARKS NEW ENGLAND HOUSE

Marcel Breuer, Architect.
George Fichera, Contractor.

Combinations of materials, so often misused, can add sparkle and interest to a crisp design when handled with the subtle restraint of this example: fieldstone is played against board and batten, glass and the strong sunshade pattern

U TILITARIAN FORMS and materials certainly no longer need justification as sensible, economical tools of design. However, placed in the knowing hands of a good architect, neither need they imply coldness or austerity. Simple devices can create fresh types of enrichment — textures, patterns, colors, and above all, constantly changing highlights and shadows—that give a delight comparable to that provided by ornaments of a past era.

The owners of this house in Andover, Massachusetts, were obviously very appreciative of this quality in Marcel Breuer's work when they commissioned him to design a new home. It was their third venture into contemporary architecture; and their previous house, which adjoins this one, was also extremely attractive.

THE NEIGHBORHOOD: Andover is a typical New England town, full of tradition and spirit. Federal and Georgian buildings face white and red brick façades onto tree-studded streets. It is primarily a quiet residential community, and one is quite soon in the hilly countryside. Inhabitants take keen interest in plays, concerts, in nearby Boston.

THE SITE: land for this house is next to the site of the Grieco's last house, which looked out under a pergola thickly hung with grape clusters. Both lots share a naturally beautiful situation with a sweeping view of the countryside. The house fits neatly into a hillside, which slopes very gently down from the road until the entrance courtyard of the house is reached, then falls away, allowing room for a lower floor.

THE FAMILY: requirements as to the amount of space and arrangement of rooms had not changed from their previous house. The Griecos are a retired business man and his wife, who have grown children, and who love gardening. They wanted their bedrooms opening onto a dressing-corridor on one side, a private terrace on the other; and a guest room with its own entrance, which could be completely separated from the rest of the house, so the children or guests could come and go at will.

THE HOUSE: the new Grieco house has a bi-nuclear plan — living and sleeping wings, separated by an entrance hall and central outdoor living terrace. The sleeping end of the house is designed according to the owners' specifications. Bedrooms open onto a yard sheltered by a low stone wall and planting. The living room is oriented toward the west to face the view. Windows are protected from the sun by an exterior louvered canopy, supported by stainless steel cables attached to four masts along the face of the building.

Guest room, bath and garage are placed on a lower floor beneath the living room, to give the required privacy and take advantage of the sloping site. Instead of a separate delivery entrance, there is a service pass-through from the entrance court into the utility room.

THE ARCHITECT: Marcel Breuer considers the house and plan to be "a good standard solution for married couples whose children are grown."

OWNERS' REACTION: Since they were admittedly very happy living in their previous house next door, Breuer's first question after being approached to plan them a new one was, "Why do you want to build another house?" The answer was simply that they admired "Breuer Architecture" so much that they wanted to experience living in it!

Details of the front of the Grieco house, shown here, are worth noting for their very effective, but completely unostentatious handling. Most windows are frameless sliding units developed by the architect. A white facia with stainless steel coping links the two wings

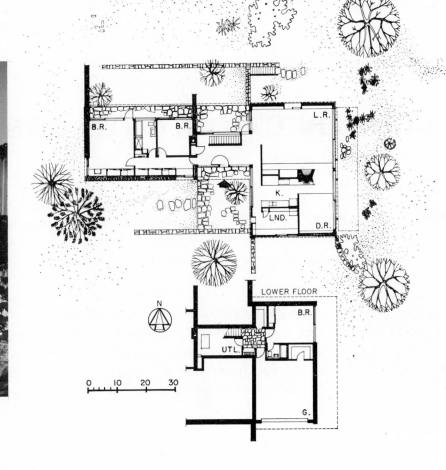

L.R.

B.R.

B.R.

K.

LND.

D.R.

LOWER FLOOR

N

B.R.

UTL.

G.

0   10   20   30

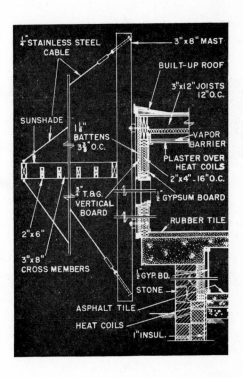

¼" STAINLESS STEEL CABLE

3"x8" MAST

BUILT-UP ROOF

3"x12" JOISTS 12" O.C.

SUNSHADE

1⅛" BATTENS 3¾" O.C.

VAPOR BARRIER

PLASTER OVER HEAT COILS

2"x4"-16" O.C.

½ GYPSUM BOARD

¾" T.&G. VERTICAL BOARD

RUBBER TILE

2"x6"

3"x8" CROSS MEMBERS

½ GYP. BD.

STONE

ASPHALT TILE

HEAT COILS

1" INSUL.

BREUER | 75

DESIGNERS & BUILDERS, ARCHITECTS. *Mr. and Mrs. Franklin E. Schaffer, Owners. Location: Greenwich, Connecticut. Leonore Baronio, Landscape Architect.*

PANEL CONSTRUCTION CUTS COST

Considerable time and money were saved in the construction of this house by the use of floor, roof and wall panels designed and built on the site by the architects. These repetitive units were fabricated on an 8 by 12-foot work table; they consist of stressed skin panels of plywood, nailed and glued to 2-inch frameworks. Exterior surfaces are textured redwood, interiors are painted. The framing module was allowed to vary, within stock plywood sizes, to fit interior space requirements.

The post and beam frame is carried on steel fins imbedded in concrete piers. The piers were formed and poured in dry-stacked, masonry chimney block. Non-solid exterior walls were glazed with plate glass or packaged sliding windows — all clipped on the exterior of the structural frame. The stressed skin panels also serve other functions. Floor panels were aluminum lined and used as ducts to insulate and heat floors. Warm air is fed through them to a perimeter duct, where floor registers direct air against the glass.

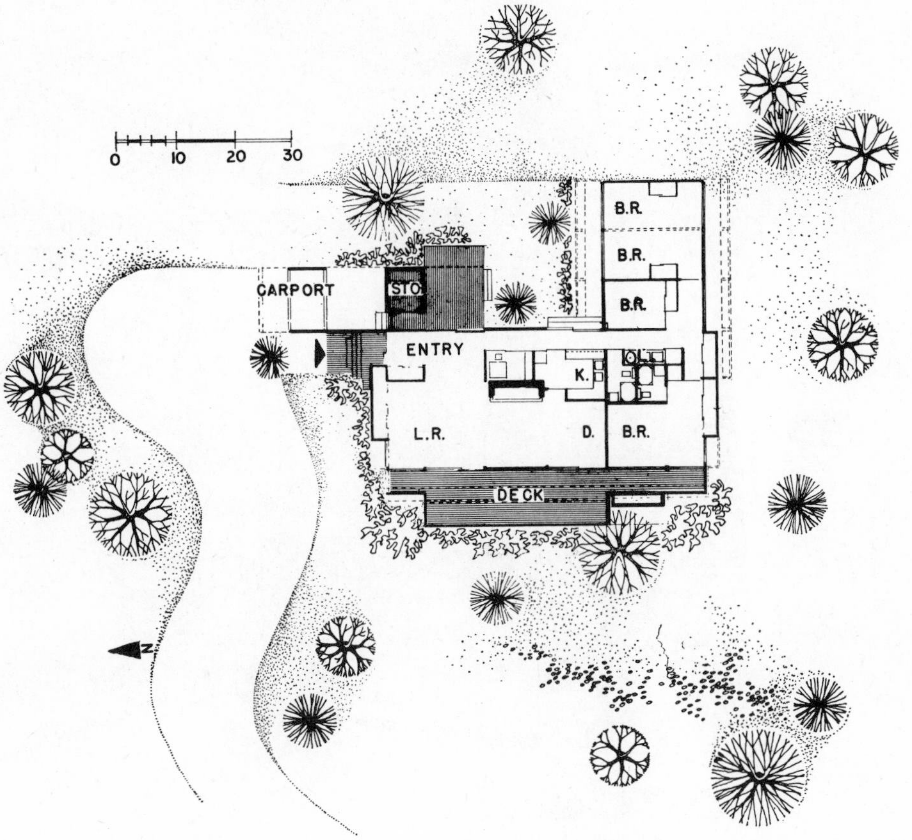
0
10
20
30
CARPORT
STO.
ENTRY
K.
B.R.
B.R.
B.R.
L.R.
D.
B.R.
DECK
N

BEN SCHNALL

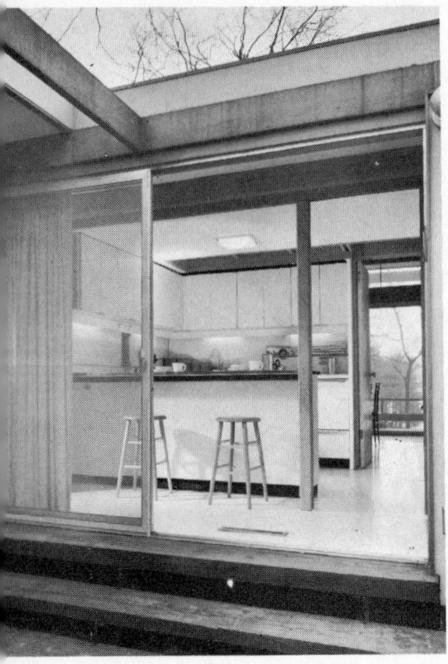

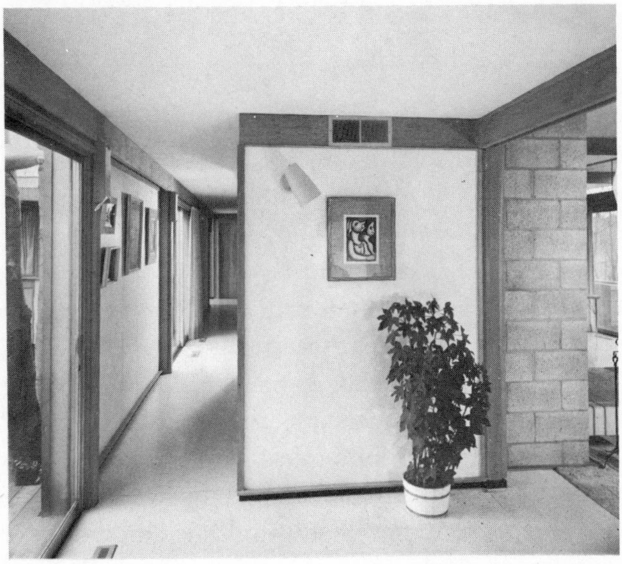

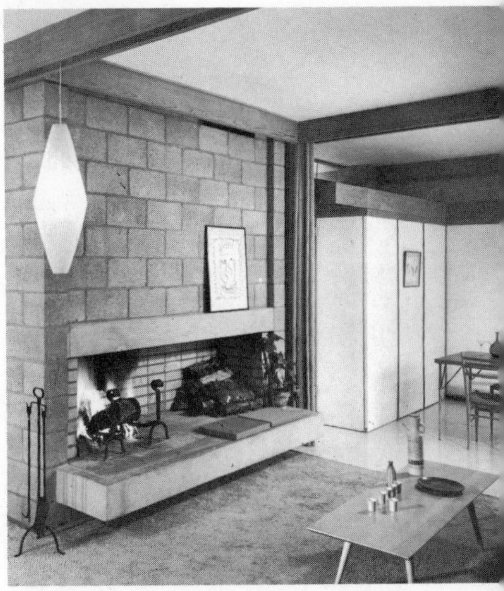

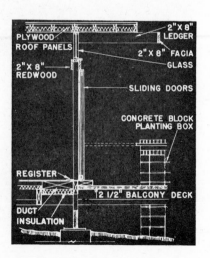

PLYWOOD
ROOF PANELS
2" X 8"
REDWOOD

2" X 8"
LEDGER
2" X 8" FACIA
GLASS

SLIDING DOORS

CONCRETE BLOCK
PLANTING BOX

REGISTER

2 1/2" BALCONY DECK

DUCT
INSULATION

The panels in the Franklin Shaffer house also contain electrical wiring, passed through voids in them and in hollow columns. Built-in lights are incorporated in the columns. All paint finishes were primed before the panels were put in place. Two large closet elements, at either side of the house, were fabricated with separate roofs and cantilevered off the ends of the framework.

In plan, the house features a number of dual-use elements. The cantilevered "closet" unit off the living area is fitted as a compact studio for painting and can be closed with sliding screens (visible at right in photo above). Sliding panels also divide the living and dining areas. A rather novel use of a folding wall permits part of the hallway off the kitchen to be used as a breakfast area (left photo p. 77). The children's bedroom is also divisible and can be rearranged for play or sleep. Services are banked to form a utility core; the laundry opens directly on the hall.

NORTH-CENTRAL

CENTRAL COURT ADDS SPACE

THE PLIGHT OF too many houses on narrow subdivision lots, is that of having to peer directly into neighboring windows across minimum setbacks. Of the many devices that architects are developing to avoid this situation, the use of a central court is growing in popularity. By facing rooms inward toward it, outside walls are freed of having to provide light and air, and can be blank, translucent — or what you will.

Probably the reason for the success of this type of plan is that it makes even a very small house seem quite spacious — a trick of the eye that has little to do with the actual area of the court. The airiness and openness that it gives can be readily seen in this small house for Mr. and Mrs. H. P. Davis Rockwell, designed by Schweikher and Elting. On three sides of the exterior, walls of major rooms are completely blank. Glass is used only at the entrance and facing the grounds at the back of the lot. But within the house, there is little sense of this enclosure — due to the court. Trees and sky have open play, and neighboring houses are blanked out of view. And the owners have complete control of the outlooks from their windows.

THE NEIGHBORHOOD: the house is located in a fairly small subdivision in Flossmoor, Illinois, which lies very near Chicago.

THE SITE: the lot is narrow and deep. There are houses on both sides, the street in front. The forward part of the lot is at street level, and a ravine cuts across the property diagonally at the back. The best exposure is southwest overlooking the ravine.

Schweikher and Elting, Architects. E. W. Sproul Construction Company, Contractors.

As a focus for all rooms in the Rockwell house, the central court serves a decorative, as well as utilitarian function. A pool, louvered grills and a minimum of landscaping create a delightful vista all year

SCHWEIKHER AND ELTING | 81

THE FAMILY: Mr. and Mrs. H. P. Davis Rockwell have three small children and "half a score of transient animals." At the outset of the planning for the house, Mr. Rockwell held a position as an engineer in a fabricating plant. After moving into the completed house, he gave up his position and went back to school at Illinois Institute of Technology to study architecture under Mies van der Rohe.

THE HOUSE: for all its openness and simplicity, the plan is well defined and works quite well. The living room, and the lower level beneath it, are placed to take advantage of the only view. Bedrooms are closed to the street side, open on the central court. Louvers and curtains give them ample privacy when needed. The lower level will ultimately be developed into guest quarters. At present it is undivided space, except for the heater room, used as a play room for the children.

Except for the large glass areas overlooking the ravine, the exterior is brick veneer. The court sides are light wood members, louvers, glass, and a third one of brick with a service gate.

THE ARCHITECTS: Paul Schweikher and Winston Elting, who now have individual firms, state that, in planning the house "there were two basic thoughts. The first — greater composure and depth within the rectilinear discipline as opposed to the wing or in-line plan. The second — control of the environment in a fairly small subdivision."

OWNERS' REACTION: the Rockwells say that "This house is good to us — it lets us live with sky, sunlight, and our woods. The inner courtyard is a serene center from any point in the house. In the summer we eat in the court, the children play there. They swim in the pool. Even in winter when we can't be in it, the court remains the core of the house."

The living area of the Rockwell house capitalizes on view of woods (below) and of the court (right). With all curtains open, woods can be seen from bedrooms. Bedroom halls and baths are illuminated by long skylights in the roof

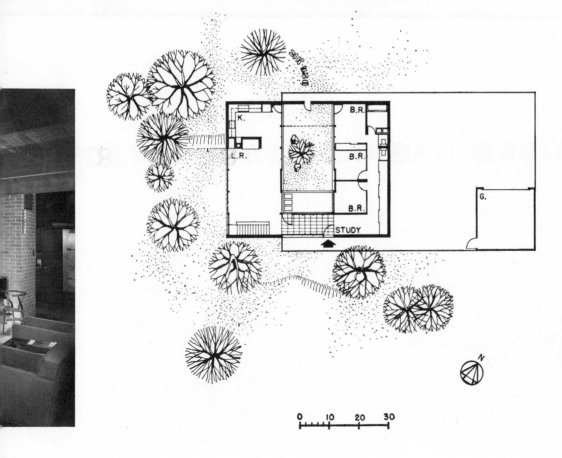

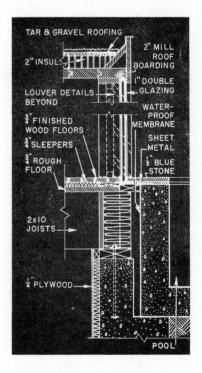

Labels in plan: K. / L.R. / B.R. / B.R. / B.R. / STUDY / G. / N

0 10 20 30

Labels in detail: TAR & GRAVEL ROOFING / 2" INSUL. / 2" MILL ROOF BOARDING / 1" DOUBLE GLAZING / LOUVER DETAILS BEYOND / WATER-PROOF MEMBRANE / ¾ FINISHED WOOD FLOORS / SHEET METAL / ¾ SLEEPERS / ½ BLUE STONE / ¾ ROUGH FLOOR / 2x10 JOISTS / ¼ PLYWOOD / POOL

SCHWEIKHER AND ELTING | **83**

YAMASAKI, LEINWEBER & ASSOCIATES, ARCHITECTS. *Mr. and Mrs. S. Brooks Barron, Owners.*
Location: Argyle Crescent, Detroit, Michigan. S. Brooks Barron, Contractor.
Edward A. Eichstedt, Landscape Architect

HEDRICH-BLESSING

CITY HOUSE HAS COUNTRY PRIVACY

This luxurious urban house has the personality, privacy, and gracious elegance of a suburban or country residence. Built in a Detroit subdivision, the house meets rigid zoning laws with good contemporary design and at the same time provides detachment from neighbors. The house is deliberately planned, by means of visual surprises, geometric patterns, and rich materials, to make walking through it and living in it an enjoyable experience.

This well-established neighborhood had zoning restrictions which made two stories and a pitched roof mandatory. The owners wanted the convenience of a one-story house. Architects Yamasaki, Leinweber and Associates met the problem by designing a two-story bedroom wing at the front of the lot and a one-story living–service wing at the rear.

From outside, the house blends quietly with the character of the neighborhood. A pierced brick wall shields the two-story brick wing with built-up roof (photo above.) It is on the inside, away from the city scene, that this house becomes architecturally exciting.

Within the brick wall of the S. Brooks Barron residence lies a half-shadowed, half-open reflecting pool (photo above). A covered walk approaches the house alongside the pool. Inside the front door a glass roof opens the entrance hall to the sky (left photo p. 86). White travertine flooring extends to the sunken area, where steps lead down into a living room overlooking a Japanese rock garden through a wall of glass (middle photo p. 86). A 3-ft. ledge around the room provides more seating space. Dining area is separated from the living room only by difference in floor level. That area, too, has a wall of glass and view of garden. The stairhall, with its 15-ft high glass wall, faces the reflecting pool. Vertical brass poles cage the stairway. Luxurious materials, such as the green and copper onyx panel above the fireplace, give rich background to the simple but elegant furnishings selected by Mrs. Barron.

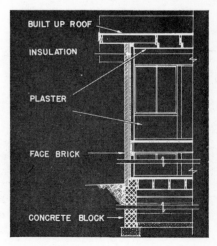

BUILT UP ROOF
INSULATION
PLASTER
FACE BRICK
CONCRETE BLOCK

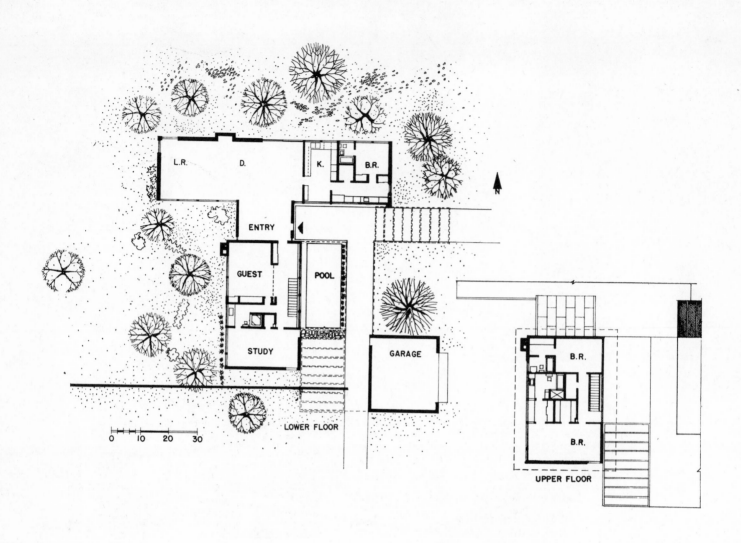

LOWER FLOOR

UPPER FLOOR

1958 Honorable Mention, National AIA Award Program

RICHARD E. BARINGER, *ARCHITECT*

Dr. and Mrs. Stanford R. Gamm, Owners.
Location: Highland Park, Illinois.
Arnold Pedersen, Contractor.
Rogers Follensbee, Heating Engineer.
Robert Zion, Landscaping Architect.

A FOUR-IN-ONE SCHEME

Privacy where needed, along with a maximum potential for indoor-outdoor living, were achieved in this house by creating well-defined zones for separation of family activities, and an harmonious balance of public and private courtyards. By joining three simple rectangular structures under one roof, four compounds were formed (children's bedrooms, parents' quarters, general living area, and garage and shop compound), each with its own courtyard. Both the children's compound and the master bedroom suite open onto private, walled-in courtyards. An outdoor terrace faces the family room.

The living, dining, and family areas flow into one space, interrupted only by the mechanical core in which is located the kitchen and utility room. From a pit in the living room, a dramatic, free-standing fireplace rises to the ceiling and sweeps through a 5-by-8-ft plastic skylight.

Courtyards, Public and Private . . .

Separation of the three rectangular units is frankly expressed by low walls running beneath the beams. Construction is post and beam on 12 ft 4 in. centers with 3 in. wood decking and a built-up roof.

Night shot shows sliding glass interior walls of the master bedroom compound leading onto a private, walled-in garden. Fireplace flue is seen extending through the living area skylight; another skylight is above the inside bath.

Plate II

BARINGER

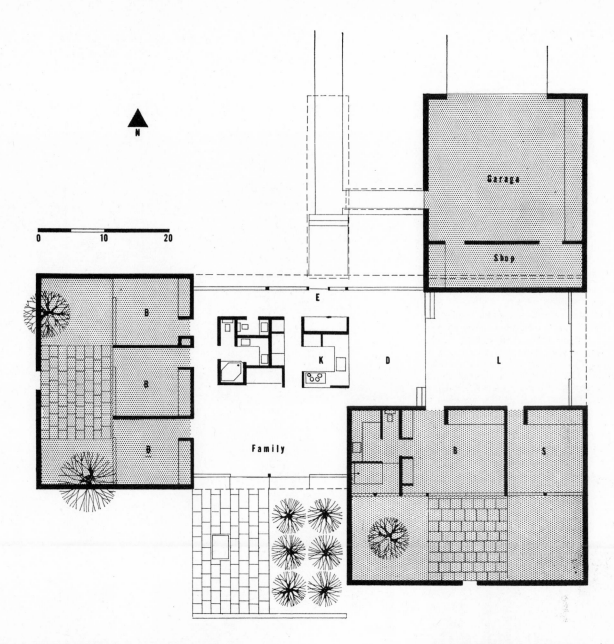

Glass doors open from master bedroom (left) onto a walled-in court-yard for private indoor-outdoor living. Here the floor is vertical cedar. Interior walls are brick and natural cedar. Other floors are terrazzo.

The kitchen (right) is open to dining area and to the public terrace where informal meals are taken and entertaining is done. The house is heated by combination forced warm and cool air in a perimeter system.

The Fireplace . . .

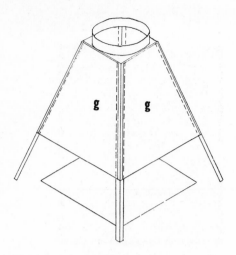

a. Plastic skylight. b. Wood cant strip. c. Plastic foam insulation covered with plastic and stainless steel collars, copper flashing. d. Guy wire and turnbuckle to stabilize flue. e. Twelve gauge, stainless steel flue, 15-in. internal diameter. f. Rotating damper. g. Porcelain panels supported on 1-in. stainless steel angles, attached to base by anchor bolts. Size of the hood is 2 ft 8 in. at the bottom of the panels, 1 ft 4 in. at top. h. Hearth in white marble. i. Firebrick. j. Ceramic tile.

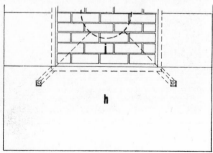

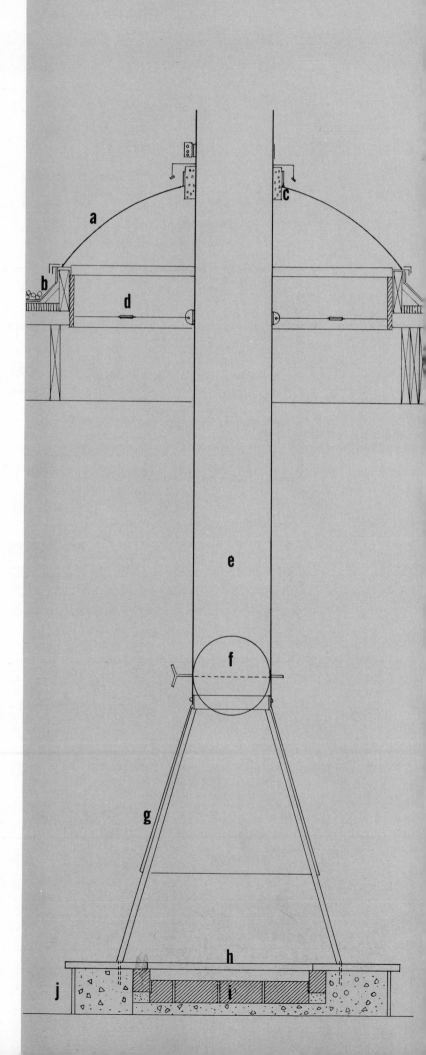

The usual household fixtures and equipment can, through creative design, be treated in unusual, interesting, and effective ways. Particular evidence can be found in the fireplace and flue construction for this house, and in the arrangement of the bathroom equipment.

To obtain the effect of an open fire beneath an open sky, the architect designed a free-standing fireplace, using standard parts, which extends through a 5- by 8-ft plastic skylight in the living room ceiling. The "open fire" was achieved by standing a porcelain-enameled steel hood, 2 ft 8 in. square at the base, over a 5- by 6½-ft raised marble hearth. The 12 gauge stainless steel flue (15-in. internal diameter) rises 6 ft to the plastic dome and extends about 3 ft beyond, where the flue is finally capped.

In the master suite bathroom, the architect has provided such luxuries as a step-down, sunken tub,

separation of the bathing, toilet, and dressing areas, and gay, theatrical lighting of the dressing room mirror. Again, he has worked with mostly standard equipment to produce an unusual and pleasant effect.

The combination tub and shower stall is of ceramic tile, and is depressed 2 ft to form a sunken area. A 2-ft ledge is left along one wall for seating. The tub itself is about 3½ ft wide. An 8-ft-high glass wall separates the tub area from the private courtyard of the master suite. Drapes can be closed for additional privacy. One-inch tubes form a curtain rod, towel bar, and handrail leading down into the tub.

Cedar partitions separate the three bathroom areas (see plan below), and yet keep the areas within a unified space for easy circulation. The dressing counter, 30 in. high, is L-shaped for extra working space and includes within it the sink and built-in cabinets. A plastic ceiling lights the entire bathroom.

And The Bathroom — Creative Design For Standard Utilities

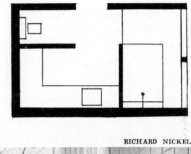

RICHARD NICKEL

HOME HAS EXPOSED STEEL FRAME

T HE PROSPECT OF BUILDING a house in the woods often creates visions of a structure straight from *Hansel and Gretel*, or at least of interiors overlaid with tanbark rusticity. In this house for Ben Rose in Highland Park, Illinois, Architectural Designer A. James Speyer has deliberately ignored all the old cliches — and with great success.

Such citified materials as steel and wide glass expanses have been used to create a house that makes living on a wooded site a constant panoramic delight. The entire house is raised on the steel columns, which have individual footings in order to disturb the natural forest landscape as little as possible.

The very simplicity of the house makes it seem quite at home in this setting; its glass walls make little interruption in the scene, and the trees, in turn, add shade and privacy. The street facade, however, is entirely of windowless wood siding, except for panels of obscure glass in the entrance loggia.

THE NEIGHBORHOOD: Highland Park, Illinois, is a suburban community near Chicago. It is generally a typical suburban arrangement of streets and lots, with houses set well back from the tree-lined streets. The architecture varies from the most traditional to modern of all kinds.

THE SITE: formerly part of a large estate, the land is in a pristine forest condition, and seems larger than its actual acreage because it borders on similar remnants of the old estate. A deep ravine edges the back of the property and increases its woodsy atmosphere.

A. James Speyer, Designer. George E. Danforth, Associated Architect. Frank Kornacker, Structural Engineer. Joseph P. Bazzoni, Mechanical Engineer. Tilander Bros., Inc., Contractor.

The living room of the Ben Rose house is virtually a steel-framed glass box, perched lightly in its wooded setting. The large room can be made as open or closed as desired by adjusting the curtains over the glass

HARRY CALLAHAN

THE FAMILY: Mr. and Mrs. Ben Rose have two young sons. Mr. Rose is a fabric designer, and required a studio-workshop to do experimental silk screen printing for his designs. The family preferred to have small bedrooms in order to afford a really large living room.

THE HOUSE: the steel frame, painted a dark Indian Red, has regular ten-foot bays. The bay width was established as a minimum size for the bedrooms. Floor and roof slabs are structural cedar decking. The cedar is left exposed as ceiling finish in most of the house. In the living room, four plaster panels form a dropped ceiling and contain radiant heating coils to augment the baseboard radiation in this large room.

In plan, the house has well defined living, sleeping and service zones, with baths and storage lining the blank facade. All baths are illuminated by skylights. Circulation is very convenient throughout. The bedroom nearest the entrance hall doubles as playroom or study for the children. The studio has sliding doors, can be joined with entry.

The living room is quite big, and its three walls of glass make it seem even larger. A free-standing fireplace and screen and curtain dividers permit a wide variety of possible furniture arrangements in the area. The lower sections of the windows open for ventilation.

THE ARCHITECTURAL DESIGNER: A. James Speyer remarks that, "The character of the house was suggested by the wooded site — a kind of 'house in the woods', simple, not too insistent, but clearly placed there, a foreign but sympathetic object in the natural surroundings."

OWNERS' REACTION: the long glass walls form ideal display and testing areas for the fabrics Ben Rose designs; and the layout gives a studio location set apart from regular family activities.

The façade of the Ben Rose house (below) gives little indication of the actual openness of the house, but lends a quiet privacy. Width of bedroom (below, left) sets standard bay width for the entire house; living room (right) is four bays wide

TOM YEE

TOM YEE

HARRY CALLAHAN

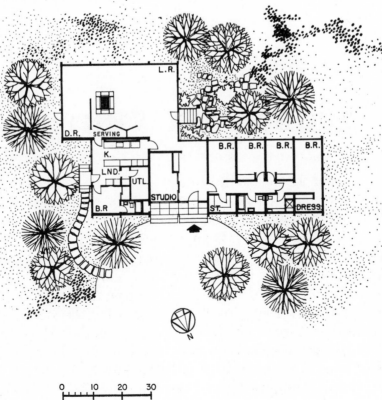

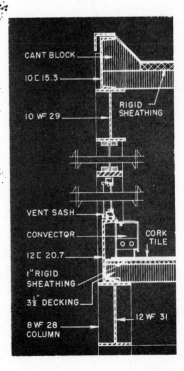

CANT BLOCK

10 ⊏ 15.3

RIGID SHEATHING

10 WF 29

VENT SASH

CONVECTOR

CORK TILE

12 ⊏ 20.7

1" RIGID SHEATHING

3½ DECKING

8 WF 28 COLUMN

12 WF 31

GEORGE NELSON & GORDON CHADWICK, ARCHITECTS

Mr. and Mrs. James T. Kirkpatrick, Owners.
Location: Kalamazoo, Michigan.
Peter Bruder, Engineer.
Thomas Smith Kelly, Lighting Consultant.
George Nelson & Co., Interior Designers.
John J. Meninga, Contractor.

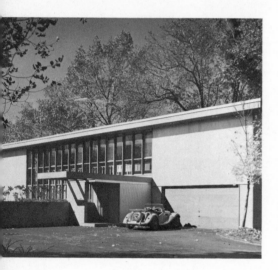  

NORMAN F. CARVER, JR.

ACCENT ON VERTICAL SPACE

In a time when the horizontal line reigns in house design, it is intriguing to note here how much visual spaciousness can be added by vistas looking *up* as well as across and out. A good sense of scale is given, too, by contrasting the verticals and horizontals. It is an interesting house, pervaded by an air of quiet elegance and warmth. Day and night, carefully planned lighting adds a touch of sparkle and drama to the interiors. The plan organization and use of durable materials add up to good livability. The first floor plan centers on a multi-purpose dining-family room, used somewhat like the traditional English "hall." An entrance vestibule with coat closet opens directly into it, as does the garage. The living room forms a quiet area at the end of the house. Upstairs, a childrens' wing is set apart with a large play room. The house is wood frame, with concrete foundations and exterior walls of ribbed aluminum panels.

Space Inside Is Well Organized . . .

Activity zones are well defined within the simple rectangular shape of this house: parents, guests, children, and noisy or quiet activities all have separate areas. All plumbing, flues and mechanical equipment are ganged for economy, and their area has brick walls for quiet. The playroom is skylighted.

The verticals of the windows and railings fill most rooms with patterns of light and shade (left). The lower photo is the stair hall between living and family rooms; above is the bedroom hall. Living room floors are slate, all others are vinyl tile.

The window bay in the living room (below) extends the full two-story height for added sense of space and light. Alcoves at either side of the living room are filled with storage units. Walls are finished in brick and plaster. Ceilings throughout the house are plaster. Jalousie windows are used for ventilation.

NORMAN F. CARVER, JR.

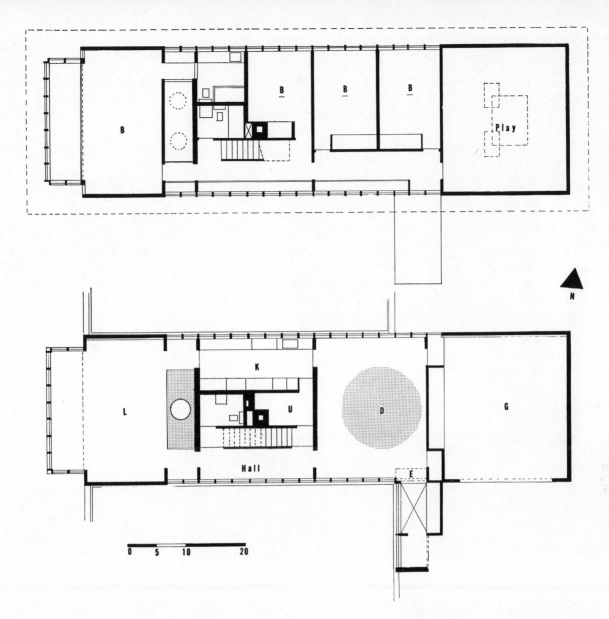

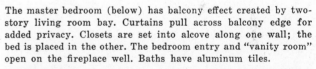

0 5 10 20

N

The hooded fireplace (below) is dramatically set in a garden-like alcove at one end of the living room. Windows at the sides and skylights above flood it with light; at night floodlights give the same effect. The fireplace is set in a bed of white pebbles, and has a round black slate hearth.

The master bedroom (below) has balcony effect created by two-story living room bay. Curtains pull across balcony edge for added privacy. Closets are set into alcove along one wall; the bed is placed in the other. The bedroom entry and "vanity room" open on the fireplace well. Baths have aluminum tiles.

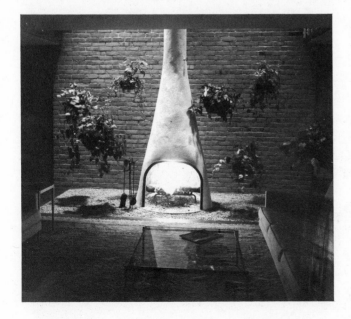

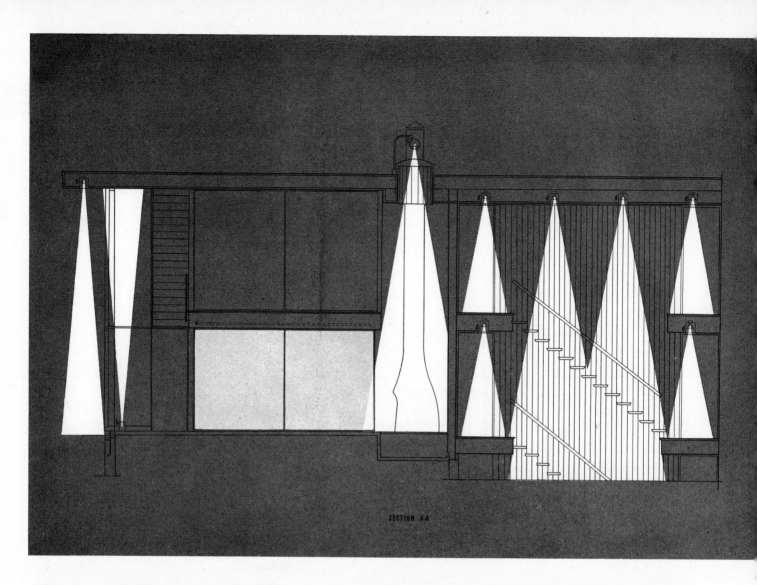

SECTION A-A

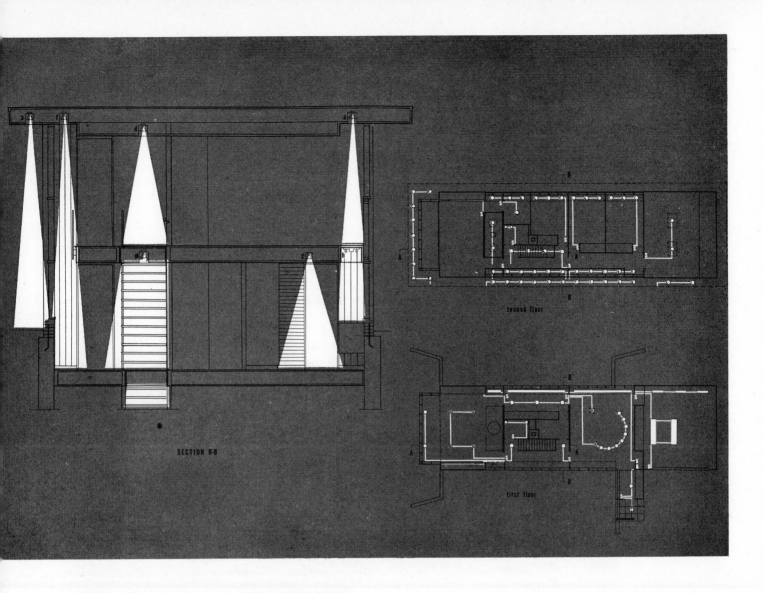

SECTION B-B

second floor

first floor

Lighting Is Used As Creative Design . . .

LEGEND
a. 75 watt spot light.
b. 150 watt up-light.
c. 300 watt weather-proof light.
d. 75 watt flood light.
e. 550 watt recessed incandescent lens strip.
f. 150 watt spot light.
g. 150 watt recessed baffled down-light.
h. 150 watt louvered fluorescent unit.

Artificial light, used as a device to explain and heighten design features, is worth notice in this house. All too often, the utilitarian niceties of lighting are the only ones given much consideration in residential design. Here, light is used as well to create an atmosphere within and without the house, and to re-create at night all the focal points around the two-story wells, as in the photograph at far left. By using only the exterior lights in the overhangs, soft illumination is provided inside; a series of lights along the stair well give utilitarian light and dramatize that feature; and with all lights on, a brilliant "party atmosphere" is created. Ceiling edges and lights are recessed where there are no actual vertical wells to give the same effect (see two photos left). Storage walls in the living room and the well are lighted in a fashion to give soft background glow. Activity areas in the multi-purpose room are defined by pools of light over tables and sofas.

GEORGE FRED KECK
WILLIAM KECK, ARCHITECTS.
Mr. and Mrs. Walter D. Gray, Owners.
Location: Olympia Fields, Illinois.
Walter D. Gray, Contractor.
R. W. Hazekamp, Landscape Architect.
Marianne Willisch, Interior Designer.

Honorable Mention, House & Home "Homes for Better Living" Competition, 1958

GERALD GARD

SLATED: THE CURTAIN WALL

The steel frame and curtain wall structure so familiar to modern office buildings has been delicately scaled down and put to residential use here. Black slate panels form part of the curtain walls, a rather unusual and effective treatment of the material. The resulting floor plan works as efficiently as that of an office and provides a setting more informal, comfortable, and elegant.

Keeping the column and beam construction as light as possible, the architects left the steel exposed—but painted it a crisp white to contrast with the exterior walls of black slate, aluminum louvers, and glass panels. By spacing the bays at regular intervals, a flexible pattern of open and closed interior areas was achieved. Separation of living and sleeping areas, always a major problem in house planning, was effected by centering the kitchen and utilities in a "buffer zone." Inside bathrooms are along a mechanical core.

Planned For Comfort And Efficiency, Like A Luxury Office . . .

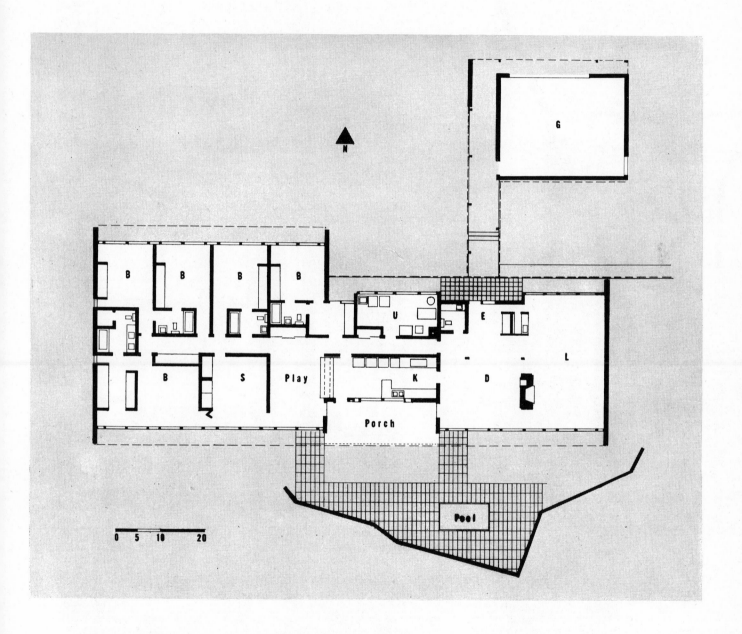

A plastic luminous ceiling brightens the long corridor (left) as well as the inside baths. The four bedrooms (below) and a master suite have built-in cabinets.

The study (below) becomes a second living room connected to the master bedroom. Interior finishes are white plaster, oak doors, walnut cabinets, and panel walls.

Mechanical vents air the kitchen (below) and baths. Equipment is built-in. Radiant hot water heating carried in copper tubes warms both the ceiling and floors.

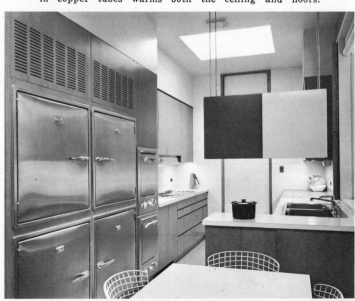

GERALD GARD

Page 104

KECK & KECK

Plate III   KECK & KECK

SOUTH

THREE UNITS SEPARATE ACTIVITIES

This extremely interesting house offers a highly original scheme for giving each segment of a family maximum privacy in its own quarters and ample space for general family living. The problems caused by limitations of a city lot and by the close proximity of neighboring houses are also well answered.

The house is built in three units, linked by glassed-in bridges at the second floor level. The unit nearest the street contains the carport, with quarters for a teenage son above. This apartment will eventually have a private entrance stair. The center unit is the major one, and includes living, dining, and service areas at the ground level, and girls' rooms, study, sewing room, and laundry on the second floor. At the back is the parents' apartment, with a shaded garden .for adults below it. A play court for the children is between the first two units. The house was planned for the parents to live in the center section when the children leave home, with the end units for visitors.

LAWRENCE, SAUNDERS & CALONGNE, ARCHITECTS.   *Dr. and Mrs. Philip M. Tiller, Jr., Owners. Location: New Orleans, Louisiana. Keller Construction Corp., Contractor. Ellzey & Estopinal, Structural Engineers. John D. Lockwood, Electrical Engineer.*

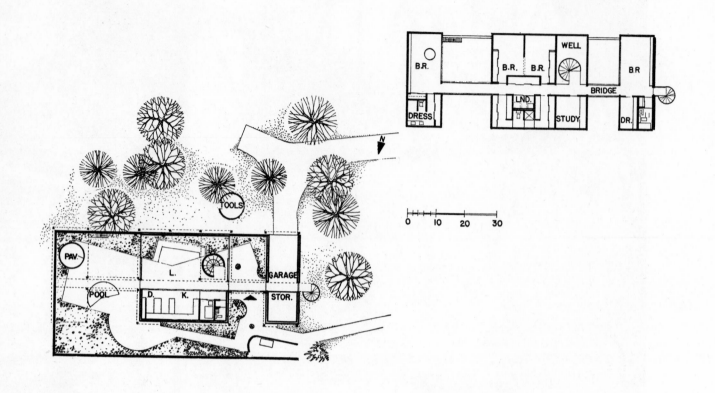

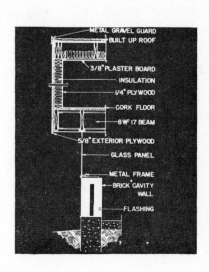

The living area of the Philip M. Tiller, Jr., house is considerably increased by the garden courts. These are defined and given privacy by simple brick walls. A "mobile mural" (above), designed and executed by John Clemmer, permits the kitchen to be completely opened to the living area, or closed-off as desired.

There are a minimum of windows facing neighboring houses, and a profusion of skylights over the second level. A unique "floor window" is also included in the master bedroom: a hole in the floor has a cowling built up to coffee table height — this is topped with glass and gives a view of the garden. The spiral staircase in the central unit also forms an eye-catching feature.

Perhaps much of the ingenuity expressed in the house was fostered by the owner. He wanted a house that "need have none of the usual norms of respectability," but be a place where he "could enjoy taking a vacation."

VICTOR A. LUNDY, ARCHITECT.
Mr. and Mrs. Samuel H. Herron, Jr., Owners.
Location: Sarasota, Florida.
Spear, Inc., Contractors.

Honor Award, House & Home "Homes for Better Living" Competition, 1959

BOLD INTERPLAY OF FORMS

The fact that a house need not necessarily be box-shaped (or any other standard form) is gaining a number of interesting adherents. With modern techniques—and the revival of some older ones—varieties of more sculptural concepts are possible. This is a good example: circles, squares and fanciful curves are deftly interlocked to form a forceful, different, and highly adaptable house. It is sheltered by a sinuous, free-standing roof of laminated glued wood arches. Beneath this, nonstructural partitions define a basically H-shaped plan with a large circular living area as its core. One leg of the H is a bedroom-sleeping area, the other leg is the utility-work area, with utility room, kitchen, maid's room and den or office. Two inset screened patios flank the living area; when sliding glass doors to these patios are opened, the entire house becomes one big, free-flowing area for living and entertaining. A circular carport at the rear (photo above) echoes the shape of the living area.

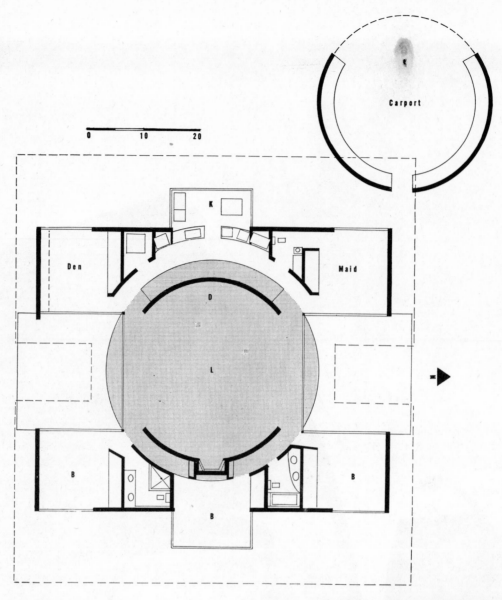

The house is planned for typical informal Florida living, offers big open areas for family and entertaining; low partitions add to sense of space.

The kitchen itself is in two compact work centers, but boasts an enormous sweep of work counter and storage cabinets, and a cheerful, glassed-in breakfast area (right). Cabinets are mahogany.

The overhanging sweep of the roof gives excellent protection from the hot summer sun, and gives sheltered outdoor sitting areas outside each room. Such a spot off the den is shown far right.

NEWHAUS AND TAYLOR, ARCHITECTS.
Mr. and Mrs. Harwood Taylor, Owners.
Developed as part of the Electri-Living Program
sponsored by Living for Young Homemakers.
Location: Houston, Texas.
Ernest Vogt, Structural Engineer.
Fred Buxton, Landscape Architect.
Lyon Development Company, Contractors.

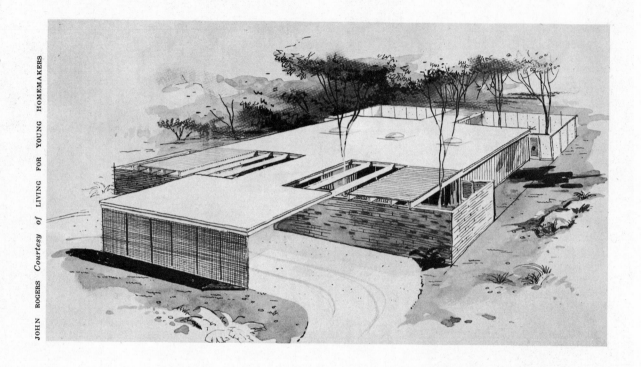

JOHN ROGERS *Courtesy of* LIVING FOR YOUNG HOMEMAKERS

First Place, Living for Young Homemakers Competition, 1958

ECONOMY IN COURTYARD HOUSE

This successful interpretation of a courtyard house grew out of the Electri-Living residential building program sponsored by *Living For Young Homemakers* together with local utility companies. Working with a mandatory budget of $18,000 or less (exclusive of lot), the architects faced a triple responsibility: to design a house at low cost which would (1) satisfy the emotional and spacial needs of an average young couple with two to four children; (2) accommodate the full electrical load of household appliances now on the market with allowances for additional equipment in the future; (3) be adaptable to the builder house market. A courtyard scheme was chosen in order to utilize all the available land space. The lot was walled-off in a rectangular shape and divided into sections, some enclosed for living areas and some left open. Space was organized to separate formal and informal living.

JOHN ROGERS *Courtesy of* LIVING FOR YOUNG HOMEMAKERS

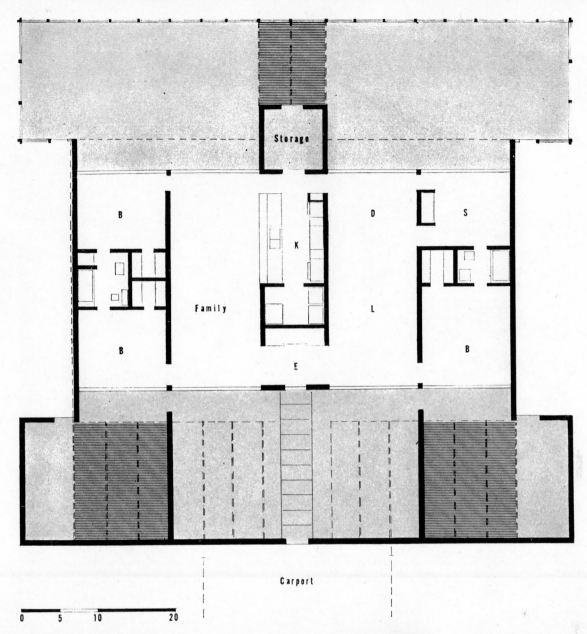

Storage

B

B

Family

K

D

S

L

B

E

Carport

0   5   10   20

The living room (photo, far left), dining room, study (or guest bedroom), and master bedroom are separated from other areas by the kitchen utility core. A wall of walnut veneer in the living room lends an air of formality to the entertaining area; other interior walls are white gypsum wallboard.

Every room has its private courtyard (photo, left center). Glass walls and doors look onto the courtyards, which are floodlit by night. Concrete and gravel surfaces in the courtyards require little upkeep. Horizontal latticework over the courts breaks the glare of the sun. Natural lighting is accomplished in kitchen and baths by use of plastic skylights.

The family and music room (photo, left) is located in the informal zone along with the children's bedrooms and bath and a party patio. Floors are surfaced with off-white terrazzo.

WALLED-IN PLAN FOR A CITY LOT

The basic concept of this attractive little house is a highly interesting one for city lots or high-density suburban areas. The entire lot is simply walled in and a glass pavilion for living quarters is set in the middle. There are no windows at all along the sides (skylights add extra light). Thus the entire lot — except for the setbacks required by the codes — becomes living space. Glass walls and outdoor areas are given complete privacy from passers-by.

The utter simplicity of the scheme and the aloofness of its almost stark walled-in front paradoxically gives the house considerable distinction and an aura of "quality." A careful selection of the few items which adorn the front wall become a public facade — coping, letterbox, light, door, and a translucent glass panel with the street address. A paved court serves as a carport. Inside the street door (which opens from the house by an electric button) there is a warm, friendly private world.

CURTIS AND DAVIS, ARCHITECTS. *Mr. and Mrs. J. T. Upton, Owners. Location: New Orleans, Louisiana.* Huger-Geer, Inc., Contractors.

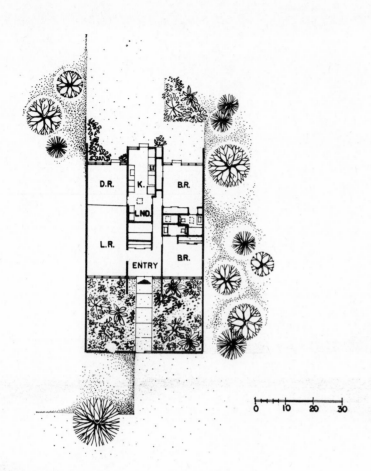

The construction of the house is as simple as its planning — and as effective. It is wood frame, with the house and front walls surfaced with natural finish cypress siding. A metal gravel guard caps the roof. Interior walls are painted plasterboard, floors, tile squares or carpet applied to a concrete slab. Glazed areas, in steel or milled cypress frames, are set back to provide protective overhangs for the major rooms. In the kitchen, the glass is brought out to the roof line to gain extra work space. The house has a year-round, gas-fired air conditioning and heating system.

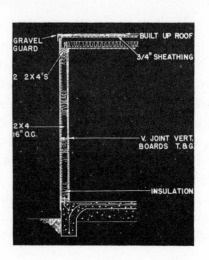

A CONTROLLED ENVIRONMENT

This colorful house by Philip H. Hiss incorporates an amazing number of new ideas, materials, and equipment within its straightforward shape: 1. The plan is zoned into four areas for privacy and noise control, divided in the center by a two-story screened court and stair hall. 2. Privacy is further assured by plastic-paneled fences, mechanically operated louvers. 3. Sound is controlled by glass fiber insulation in walls and ceiling, acoustical plaster ceilings, carpets and draperies, and air conditioning—which allows house to be closed up. 4. The building is modular, with 14- by 21-ft bays (center one is 21 by 21). The basic module is 3½ ft, the width of the sliding aluminum windows, doors and screens. 5. Construction is durable and fireproof—frame, bar joists and studs are steel. Floors are beige quarry tile on concrete slabs. The roof is steel decking, marble chips. Walls are ceramic brick, blue aluminum.

PHILIP H. HISS

PHILIP H. HISS, DESIGNER.

Mr. and Mrs. Philip H. Hiss, Owners.
Location: Sarasota, Florida.
Air Engineering, Inc., Heating Engineers.
Kenneth D. Brumbaugh, Electrical Engineer.
Phil Hall, Interior Designer.
Philip Hiss Associates, Inc.,
and A. J. Twitchell, Contractors.

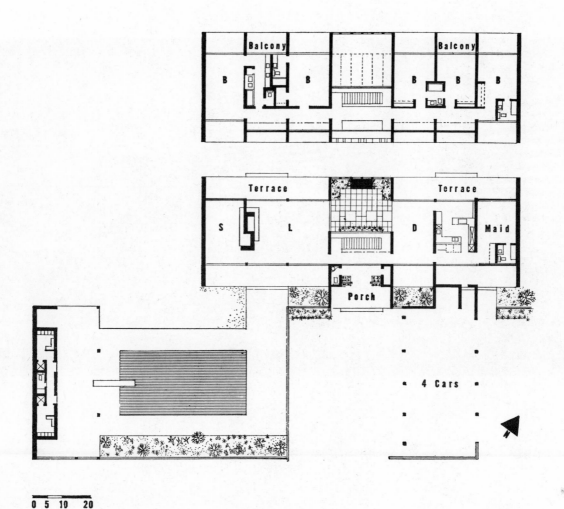

The house is planned for the automobile. A large carport has eight upward-acting doors, serves as porte cochère, with easy access to front and service entrances. The motor court gives a fine sense of "arrival" at the house, space for parking.

In the living room (top left), as elsewhere in the house, all materials and surfaces are extremely easy to keep. Walls are plaster (all paint is scrubbable), woodwork is oiled teak, floors are beige quarry tile. Predominant colors of the house are blue, green, natural wood, white and dark gray. Fireplace is mosaic.

Courts and terraces abound throughout the house: small courts are off dining and living rooms (far left), a large one in the center (middle left), and one for the pool. Each room has at least one terrace or balcony. There is ample storage—cabinets line the upstairs corridor. Built-ins have plastic surfaces.

The stairway (left) forms decorative feature at entry, has travertine treads, iron railing. Lighting throughout the house was carefully planned by the owner, has low voltage and mercury dimmer controls. The house is extremely well equipped with mechanical appliances—all possible are built-in.

ALEXANDRE GEORGES

THE SCREENED-IN FLORIDA ROOM

This house makes the most of an idea rapidly gaining popularity in balmy Florida. Often called the 'Florida Room," it consists of a large, screened, insect-free area to supplement living space during all but a brief portion of the year. Here, the idea is pursued to a near ultimate. Screened terraces, lawns and gardens flank the house and about treble its size. With sliding walls open, the entire structure is one huge screened porch — exotic, but comfortably pleasant in a warm climate.

From the outside, the house has a unified and relatively closed appearance: horizontal louvers along the front (photo above), plastic screen across the back, and solid end walls of yellow-painted concrete block. Inside, the effect is one of extreme openness (see photo, right, of the back terrace). Lush plants and grass continue in from the absolute outdoors, and help visually minimize the protecting screen. Circulation between living and service quarters and the bedrooms is via a covered walk in the front loggia.

RUFUS NIMS, ARCHITECT. *John H. Messmore, owner. Location: Redington Beach, Florida. Alois Steinwachs, Contractor*

ALEXANDRE GEORGES

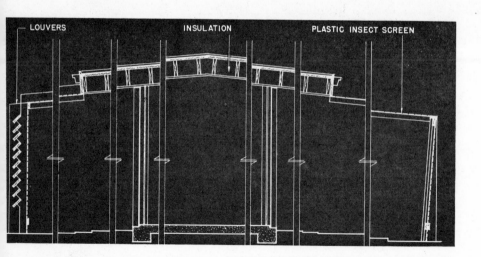

LOUVERS   INSULATION   PLASTIC INSECT SCREEN

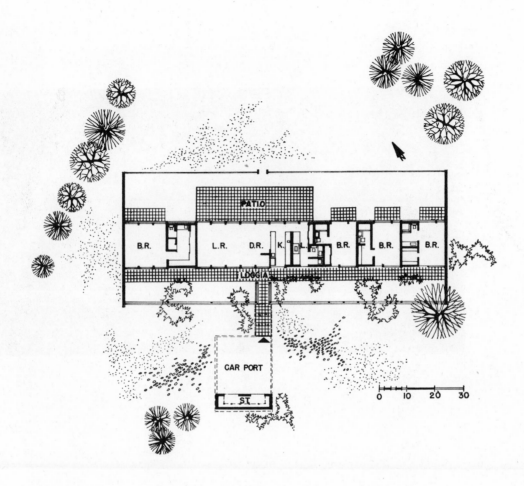

The plan of the John H. Messmore house is arranged with bedrooms for the children at one end of the house, the parents' bedroom at the other. Each room has its own bath. Living, dining, and service rooms are at the center of the house, and allow for inside circulation. Walls have alternate panels of glass and sliding jalousies, which can be closed in bad weather. All ceilings are sand-finished plaster with imbedded radiant heating cables. The roof structure has wood joists spanning between rigid steel bents on square steel columns. The section (far left) shows screen extensions.

IN THE TROPICAL TRADITION

The great sloping roof and screen façade of this contemporary conception of a traditional Florida house provide excellent shelter against tropical rains and temperatures. The two main elements of the house can be sealed tight during bad weather—or opened on nice days to create one large, screened-in area.

The problems inherent in the semi-tropics (hot sun, high tides, heavy winds, and insects) were solved in much the same manner as in the old Florida house or Seminole chikee house: a concrete platform, impervious to insects, is raised off the ground to form the floor of the house, under which may pass both high tides and cool breezes. The platform is sealed entirely at its edge with insect screening. Porches skirt the perimeter of the platform and divide the two weather-sealed areas that compose the living and bedroom elements. The effect is one of having a courtyard in the center of and surrounding the house.

ROBERT B. BROWNE, ARCHITECT.
Mr. and Mrs. Kenneth McClave, Owners.
Location: Key Biscayne, Miami, Florida.
Hugh H. McCallum, Engineer.
Warren S. Burkholder, Contractor.
Robert B. Browne and G. Cory Millican, Interior Designers.

Honorable Mention, House & Home "Homes for Better Living" Competition, 1959

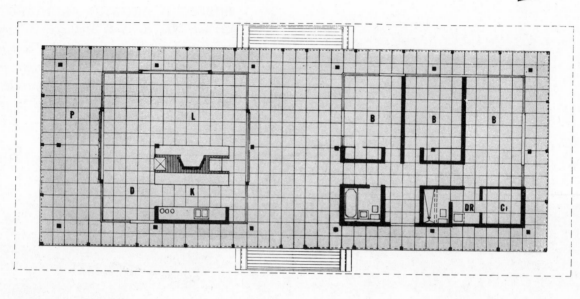

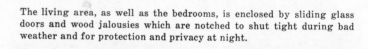

0   5   10   20

Rough-sawn pine beams and rafters, bleached to a silvery-gray tone, are left exposed throughout the house. Bedroom windows are louvered, can be opened to admit morning sun.

The living area, as well as the bedrooms, is enclosed by sliding glass doors and wood jalousies which are notched to shut tight during bad weather and for protection and privacy at night.

When sliding doors and jalousies are open, the porch becomes part of the living and bedroom areas, and a breeze flows freely through the house. Eighteen great pine posts, bleached the same silvery gray as the beams and rafters, support a roof which projects down and out on all sides for wind and rain protection. The roof surface is a highly reflective coral chip which, together with ocean breezes, provides effective year-round air conditioning. The surface of the raised platform —which serves as the floor—is polished cement tile.

Open For Breezes Or Closed For Privacy . . .

Small Galley Kitchen Yields Maximum Working Space...

A galley kitchen as well planned as this one can allow a maximum amount of working space within a small area, save steps and time involved in cooking and other kitchen operations, and integrate heavy and sometimes hard-to-fit equipment. The simple plan places cabinets, sinks, counters and equipment along two parallel walls set 8 ft apart.

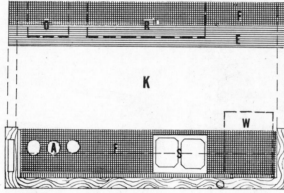

KITCHEN PLAN SHOWING LOCATION OF EQUIPMENT

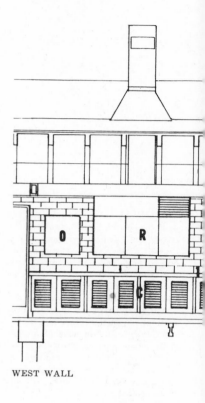

WEST WALL

An aisle width of 3 ft 6 in. makes it convenient to turn from counter to counter while working. Although there is not enough room to dine in the kitchen (except for light snacks), the dining area is easily accessible. All cabinets and storage areas are louvered for ventilation to keep food from molding. Touch-latch hardware is used on all cabinet doors. Shelves are adjustable. The floor is composed of 2- by 2-ft precast cement tiles.

Arrangement of the equipment in this kitchen expedites normal cooking procedures. The oven, built into a brick wall, is located only a few steps from the dining area so that food can be served piping hot direct from the stove. The refrigerator is nearby, also above the counter and at eye level. Electrical plates and sink are across the aisle. Food, then, can be moved easily from refrigerator to sink to oven or stove.

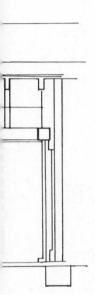

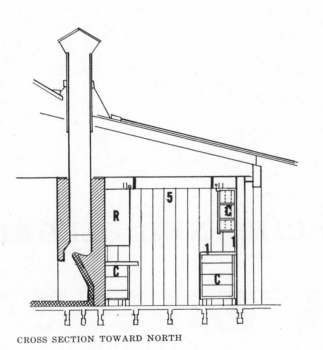

CROSS SECTION TOWARD NORTH

Two ceramic tile counters, one with a cutting board edge, run the full length of the kitchen. Cabinets and equipment are raised 1 ft above the counters to free their full 1 ft 6 in. width for working space. The lighting is indirect, done with fluorescent strips under redwood valances. Natural light passes over the partitions.

LEGEND:
A. Electric plates. C. Cabinets. D. Eight-in. drawers on nylon slides. E. Cutting board edge. F. Tile counter. O. Oven. R. Refrigerator. S. Sink. T. Tray rack. W. Automatic dish washer. 1. Ceramic mosaic tile. 2. Mexican brick wall. 3. Louvered wood doors. 4. Painted wood doors. 5. Redwood beam.

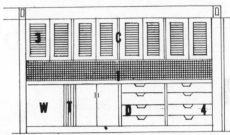

EAST WALL

Burner units are built into the ceramic mosaic tile counter. Switches and plugs are on the wall where they are easy to see and reach. A galvanized metal wiring gutter is beneath burner units for protection. The height of the tile and cutting board counter is 2 ft 2 in., which situates the working area comfortably at arm's length. The draining board counter is slightly higher (3 ft) to compensate for the recessed sink.

The ceramic mosaic tile scheme is carried through the bathroom and dressing room. Sink and fixtures are built in. Drawers below the counter top are handy for towel and linen storage. A full-length panel of wood jalousies backs the dressing counter and mirror. A plastic skylight admits more natural light to the dressing area.

DISCIPLINED ELEGANCE

1956 Medal of Honor, Houston Chapter AIA;
1956 Honor Award, Texas Society of Architects;
1956 Special Mention, House & Garden.

Bolton and Barnstone, Architects. Walter P. Moore, Structural Engineer. Thomas D. Church, Landscape. Knoll Planning Unit, Consultant on Interior Design. Van Cleve Construction Co., D. S. Rogers, Contractors.

Spacious, two-story living area gives great dramatic impact to this Houston house (see color plate IV). Relatively low ceilings in other parts of the house, and regular emphasis of a 4-foot module tend to heighten the effect

As a word, "ELEGANCE" is too often indiscriminately used — and currently somewhat out of favor — but it represents, as no other, a quality that many privately yearn for in their homes. And it is a quality sometimes bemoaned as singularly lacking these days.

This Houston, Texas, home for Mr. and Mrs. Gerald S. Gordon is an excellent answer to that argument. It is very much in the "grand manner," translated into a completely modern idiom. Architects Bolton and Barnstone have followed an overall concept which closely integrates structure and design, and have paid unusual attention to the refinement of details. Though very disciplined and understated, the end effect is far from mechanistic, and gives the impression of considerable luxury. Simple landscaping, furnishings add to this same feeling.

THE NEIGHBORHOOD: the house is in an urban residential section of Houston. Homes are conservative, largish, lawns well tended. Lots are average to moderately large in size, dotted with trees. Houstonians tend to combine western informality with deep-southern ways.

THE SITE: the house is on a fairly typical city lot, except, perhaps, for sides which slope in slightly toward the back. It is quite flat, with several nice trees. Neighboring houses are close by.

THE FAMILY: Mr. and Mrs. Gordon are a young couple with a growing family. The architect says of them, "It isn't often that we find clients who are so anxious to get a good house, that they slow you up, to give you the opportunity to reflect on what's been drawn on paper."

Plate IV   BOLTON AND BARNSTONE

THE HOUSE: structurally, the house consists of a very simple steel frame, set on a concrete slab. The five bays are filled with glass or pinkish brick panels, with the steel left exposed, painted white. All is planned on a four-foot module. Overhangs are encompassed in the overall shape of the building by insetting the glass areas.

The front of the house is serene and private; a long brick wall, with louvered black gate, extends from the steel-framed garage to enclose a generous entrance court. The neatly geometric block of the house, and trees in the court, are partially visible behind the wall.

Room relationship in the plan is very good. There is ample area for entertaining, and considerable privacy in the quiet, carpeted atmosphere of the bedroom wing. All bedrooms are furnished to double as sitting rooms. Circulation, though generally good, seems a bit circuitous from the service area to other parts of the house.

All utilities, downspouts, ducts, grilles, etc., are fitted unobtrusively into the structure, which has year-round air conditioning.

THE ARCHITECTS: on the design of this house, Bolton and Barnstone comment, "We feel that the lesson a young practitioner should always keep in mind is that new form evolves after a generation of trying — and not with the first or the fifth attempt. And if, after a generation of work something new has been added to the architectural vocabulary — that will make it all worth having done. One should keep in the main stream of a moving and evolving tradition."

OWNERS' REACTION: the Gordons remark that "We feel we are living in a piece of sculpture, unique in that it is spacious, comfortable, sparkling, and above all — beautiful."

Although the structure of the Gordon house is clearly stated and exposed, it does not dominate or overwhelm the overall design. End walls are solid to give privacy from neighbors. Similar colors and materials are used inside and out, as in foyer (below)

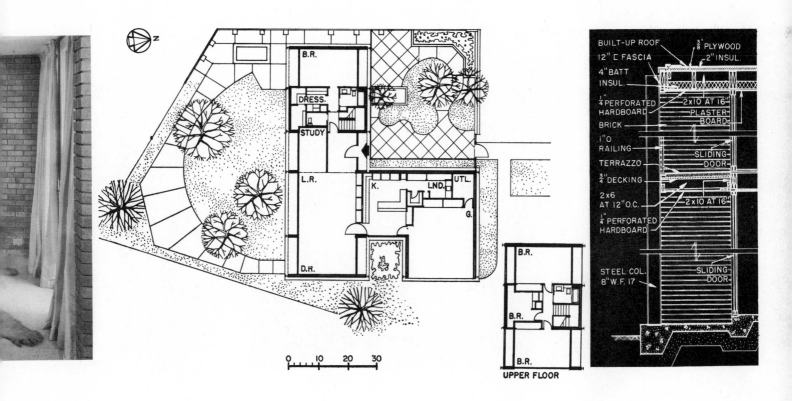

BUILT-UP ROOF
12" ⊏ FASCIA
4" BATT INSUL.
1/4" PERFORATED HARDBOARD
BRICK
1"Ø RAILING
TERRAZZO
3/4" DECKING
2×6 AT 12"O.C.
1/4" PERFORATED HARDBOARD
STEEL COL. 8" W.F. 17

3/8" PLYWOOD
2" INSUL.
2×10 AT 16"
PLASTER-BOARD
SLIDING DOOR
2×10 AT 16"
SLIDING DOOR

B.R.
DRESS.
STUDY
L.R.
K.
LND.
UTL.
G.
D.R.

B.R.
B.R.
B.R.
UPPER FLOOR

0 10 20 30

BOLTON AND BARNSTONE | 139

All of the major bedrooms in the Gordon house have balconies, sliding glass walls at each end, and are furnished as sitting rooms. Details, even in kitchen and bath are carefully studied. Bath counters are marble, amply sized

FRED WINCHELL

OPEN PLAN, PREFAB UNITS CUT COSTS

OPEN PLAN, PREFAB UNITS CUT COSTS

CONTEMPORARY MATERIALS and techniques often go a long way towards helping produce the "most house for the least money." This spacious and airy house on Siesta Key, Sarasota, Florida is composed almost entirely of prefabricated parts—which helped keep the cost moderate.

Besides the wide variety of manufactured items commonly used in houses today, Architect Paul Rudolph has also employed ready-made girders and panels for walls and roof. The panels are of a "sandwich" construction, with a honeycomb core of phenolic-impregnated paper, and hardboard or plywood of various types glued to either side; they resist fire, decay and termites, and are lightweight enough to serve as sliding doors in several locations. The girders span 32 feet across the living room, and are of a "stressed-skin" type, formed of plywood glued to light wood members.

The roof is constructed in two levels, with the upper one supported atop the beams. The lower roof panels project 6 feet into the room and are suspended from the beams; to the outside, they project as a 4-foot overhang, either cantilevered or attached by pins to sides of wooden posts. Spaces between beams form a clerestory for extra light, air.

THE NEIGHBORHOOD: Sarasota, on the west coast of Florida, is a quiet, sun-drenched land of palms and palmettos with a balmy climate.

THE SITE: ample in size and level, the lot adjoins a bayou and abounds in tropical trees and foliage. An artificial inlet has been made in the bayou to bring it to the perimeter of the house at the back.

Paul Rudolph, Architect. Harold Pickett, Monostructure, Inc., Contractor.

This very attractive and spacious house for Mr. and Mrs. David Cohen was built at moderate cost by using new structural techniques ("sandwich" panels, plywood girders) and a very open plan for living areas (preceding page, and photo below left)

THE FAMILY: Mr. and Mrs. David Cohen are an extremely musical couple. He is concert master for the Florida West Coast Symphony, and she is a pianist. They wanted a house that would accommodate large groups for rehearsals and recitals, and with good acoustics and sound system. From the design standpoint, they asked for a simple, straightforward, practical house that required a minimum of housekeeping.

THE HOUSE: the plan of the house works ideally for informal, servantless living, as well as the family's specific requirements. By eliminating all partitions except those of the bedrooms and baths, an enormous multi-purpose living area was created for entertaining or orchestra practice sessions. Even the kitchen is a part of the room; cabinets are arranged to shield the actual cooking processes from view. Sliding windows and doors join terraces at the front and back to the living area.

Large closets and a dressing room (well lighted by overhead skylights) minimize the need for excess furniture in the bedrooms, permit them to be used as sitting rooms on occasion.

THE ARCHITECT: Paul Rudolph remarks that, "Perhaps the most interesting feature of the house is the sunken area in the living room which is surrounded by cushions on the floor and additional cushions for back supports. We are much interested in the simplification and elimination of furniture and this seems to be a step. We feel strongly that too much modern furniture is so sculpturesque that it is difficult to make a truly quiet room."

OWNERS' REACTION: the Cohens muse that, "The house is right. Not fancy — very ample and straightforward — practical — not ornate — no lost space, NONE — no silly walls with curves or dead end rooms."

The entire periphery of the Cohen house is surrounded by brick paving, which serves as walks and living terraces, reduces garden upkeep. Interior finishes of plywood, hardboard, terrazzo, make housekeeping simple. Meals can be served directly from the kitchen over the low cabinet behind sink (below)

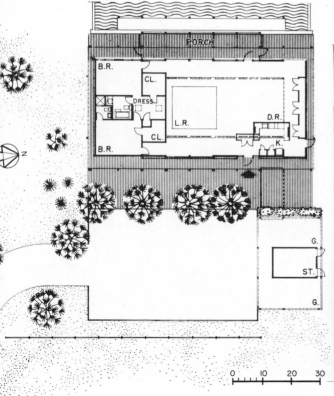

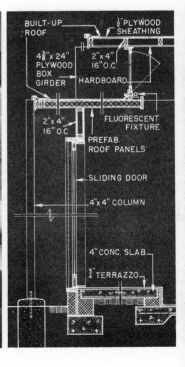

BUILT-UP ROOF

½" PLYWOOD SHEATHING

4⅜" x 24" PLYWOOD BOX GIRDER

2" x 4" 16" O.C.

HARDBOARD

2" x 4" 16" O.C.

FLUORESCENT FIXTURE

PREFAB. ROOF PANELS

SLIDING DOOR

4" x 4" COLUMN

4" CONC. SLAB

¾" TERRAZZO

PORCH

B.R.

CL.

DRESS

L.R.

D.R.

CL.

B.R.

K.

G.

ST.

G.

0   10   20   30

RUDOLPH | 145

ARCHITECTS DESIGN COMPLETE HOME

Ｎｏｗ ａｎｄ ｔｈｅｎ, one happens on a house that seems all-of-a-piece. All things about it seem to fit into a complete, unified whole — grounds, landscaping, furnishings, accessories, and the structure itself. This rarely happens unless there is a close sympathy of understanding between those responsible for the execution of each part.

In this Shreveport, Louisiana, residence for Mr. and Mrs. James Muslow, the architects did everything — planning, designing or selecting every detail. The extremely attractive result certainly justifies the owners' trust in them. In fact, the Muslows instigated the arrangement: "After discussing the situation at great length and after several weeks of trips to the furniture stores, and endless searches through brochures, we reached an important conclusion. Since our architects had congealed our ideas and their plans into a house which so satisfied us, why not take the rest of the problem to them? This decision proved a wise one, for we enjoy the house more each day."

Ｔｈｅ Ｎｅｉｇｈｂｏｒｈｏｏｄ: the area is slightly rolling, wooded, strewn with azaleas and other flowering shrubbery. Curved streets have little heavy traffic, and are lined with newish houses, broad lawns. The town's way of life mixes Louisiana traditions with a goodly leavening of some of the bustle of nearby Texas.

Ｔｈｅ Ｓｉｔｅ: slightly elevated from the street, the plot has very gentle variations in grade, and boasts a profusion of beautiful trees, mostly tall stately pines. It posed no particular problems.

Samuel G. Wiener and William B. Wiener & Associates, Architects. Robert Neff, Contractor.

Identical materials were used inside and out to enhance the unified feeling of the house. A solid stone wall faces the street, glass walls look on gardens. Understated furnishings increase decorative importance of the structural materials used

THE FAMILY: the owners have two teen-age children — son and daughter. All are interested in outdoor living and entertain extensively; a basic requirement was a plan permitting parents to entertain without interfering with the routine living of the children, and vice-versa. As a hub for this, they wanted a many-purpose family room, which would serve as a lounge, a guest room, a dressing room for the pool, and a buffet-service area for outdoor functions.

THE HOUSE: the basic structure is a simple rectangle, with occasional fin-like wall projections, and a roof cut-out section over the breakfast room court to prevent a boxy appearance. The plan meets the family requirements quite well, with two areas for dining, two for entertaining, bedrooms at the back. If circulation seems a bit circuitous at first glance, note that the main family entrance is off the garage, while the "front door" is principally for guests. The family room is well placed for its many functions, and, together with the breakfast room, can be joined with other living areas for entertaining large groups on special occasions.

THE ARCHITECTS: Samuel G. Wiener and William B. Wiener & Associates have taken careful note of the clients' tastes. "The owner requested the use of rustic type materials. It was, therefore, decided to use Colorado stone walls, random gray-green slate floors, and exterior walls of mahogany." The same materials are used on the interiors.

OWNERS' REACTION: "We are sure that architects are, also, self-made psychiatrists, because they were able somehow to take all the disjointed ideas we had thrown at them and developed the house we wanted — structure, furnishings and landscaping."

Family room, terrace and pool form central activity area for the Muslow house. Note in the photograph at right how closely these areas are integrated by wall and roof extensions, and also how much privacy they give to the adjoining rooms

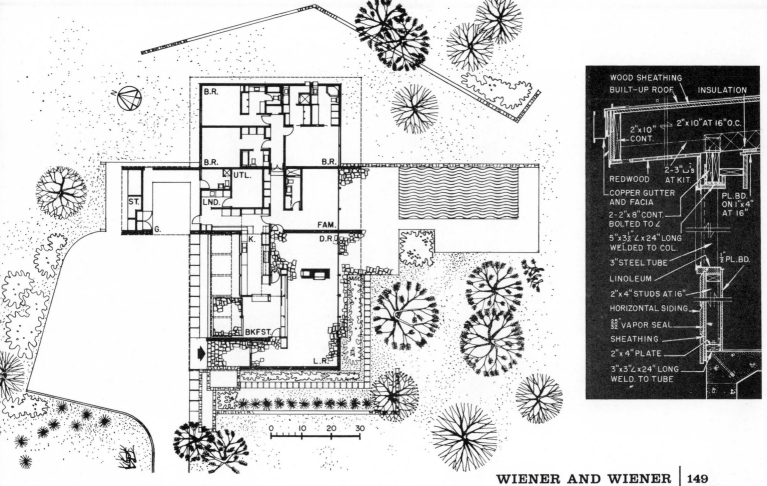

WOOD SHEATHING
BUILT-UP ROOF   INSULATION

2"x10"   2"x10" AT 16"O.C.
CONT.

                    2-3"∠'s
REDWOOD   AT KIT.

COPPER GUTTER   PL.BD.
AND FACIA   ON 1"x4"
2-2"x8" CONT.   AT 16"
BOLTED TO ∠

5"x3½"∠x24" LONG
WELDED TO COL.

3" STEEL TUBE   ½ PL.BD.

LINOLEUM

2"x4" STUDS AT 16"

HORIZONTAL SIDING

2½/32" VAPOR SEAL

SHEATHING

2"x4" PLATE

3"x3"∠x24" LONG
WELD. TO TUBE

A garden court serves as an attractive separation between the Muslow motor court and the kitchen and breakfast areas. A pass-through simplifies service in the breakfast room

FRANK LOTZ MILLER

GEORGE MATSUMOTO, ARCHITECT *and owner. Location: Raleigh, North Carolina. Frank Walser, Contractor.*

1957 Award of Merit, National AIA Award Program;
1957 Award of Merit, AIA, House & Home, Better Homes & Gardens, and NBC Award Program

DETAILS ENHANCE A SMALL HOUSE

This good looking little house stands as vital proof that standard stock materials and equipment can — with care, thought, and a knowing touch — be combined to make a fresh, unstereotyped structure. The result has warmth and elegance of finish, and the cost was amazingly low. In plan, the house works extremely well, with a maximum of living space and as little waste as there is in the structure.

The success of the house lies, no doubt, in the meticulous attention given to each tiny detail — for itself, and for its relation to the overall scheme. Each item dovetails with the next in a logical coordinated manner, yet retains individuality through contrasts of natural color, texture, and patterns of the materials.

The main impact of the house is one of lightness and suspension. This is created by cantilevering the house over its raised basement on all four sides, so that it has a modified cross shape. And it is emphasized by glass fillers between all girders.

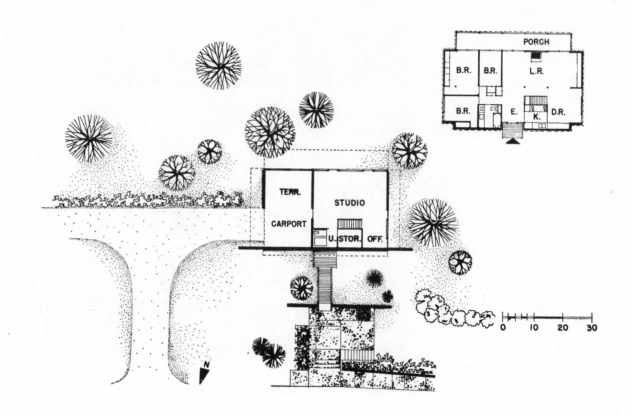

PORCH

B.R. | B.R. | L.R.

B.R. | E. | K. | D.R.

TERR.
CARPORT
STUDIO
U. | STOR. | OFF.

N

0 10 20 30

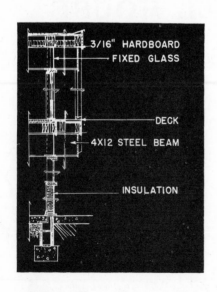

3/16" HARDBOARD
FIXED GLASS

DECK
4X12 STEEL BEAM

INSULATION

MATSUMOTO

Plate V

The George Matsumoto house has a precise post and beam structure, laid out in regular eight-foot bays. In the living area, free-standing posts and the exposed beams suggest divisions for different activities. Rich, warm wood and plywood surfaces abound throughout the house to counterbalance the precision of the structure.

The plan also combines practicality with out-of-the-ordinary features. Utilities are conveniently located, and are close together to minimize plumbing — kitchen and bath straddle the utility room on the lower floor. Traffic patterns through the house are fairly direct and unencumbered; the bedroom hall is a near minimum.

For the less usual side, there is the delightful entrance court (see photograph on page 151) with its patterned planting beds and gentle ramp up to the recessed front door. The entry gives privacy to most of the living-dining area, and focuses attention on a vista of the back garden as one comes in the house.

AECK ASSOCIATES, ARCHITECTS.
Mr. and Mrs. Howard H. Callaway, Owners.
Location: Harris County, Georgia.
T. Z. Chastain, Structural Engineer.
Lazenby & Borum, Mechanical Engineers.
Newman Construction Co., Contractor.
E. L. Daugherty, Landscape Architect.
Ben Tigner, Interior Designer.

GABRIEL BENZUR

A HOUSE OF LINKED PAVILIONS

This spacious, livable country house consists of three zoned units, linked by glassed-in galleries. One zone contains living and recreation areas; the second has service and guest quarters; the last is made up of family bedrooms. The wide galleries double as a dining area, and a family room. Each room is oriented to take advantage of views from the spectacular mountain top site. The house is located on the edge of a ridge known as "Pine Mountain," and overlooks the thousands of acres of the Ida Cason Callaway Gardens. The gardens, open to the public, are carefully cultivated sanctuaries of forest scenes, flowers, lakes and canals; the owner of the house, Howard H. Callaway, is Executive Director of the gardens. Stone for the house, of subtle yellow and orange colors, was quarried near the site. The casual, unaffected contemporary design incorporates high ceilings and a great sense of space.

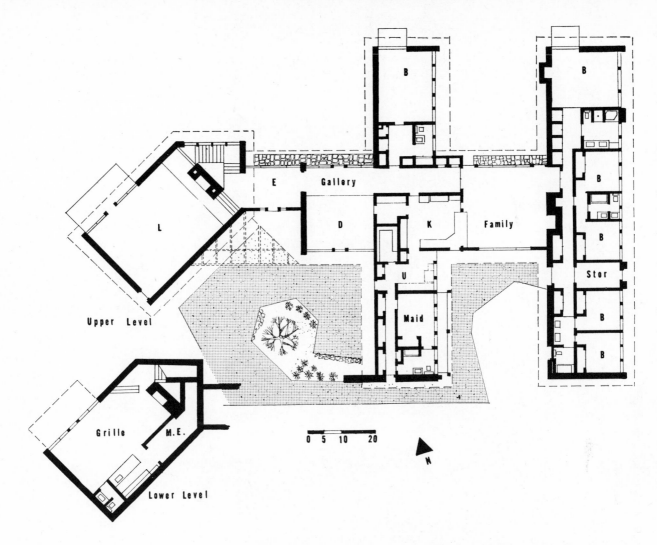

Upper Level

Lower Level

Grille   M.E.

E   Gallery

D   K   Family

U

Maid

B

B

B

B

Stor

B

B

0 5 10 20

N

Plan Divisions Give Openness and Privacy . . .

Below: the kitchen has a long breakfast counter opening directly on the family room. The opposite side of the room is a sitting area. The kitchen has plastic counters, metal cabinets, built-in range and ovens; plaster walls, and vinyl plastic tile floors.

Below: the master bedroom (as well as the guest room and living room) has a private balcony. Windows are sliding and fixed steel sash; those in baths and kitchen are wood sliding sash. All have built-in screens. A built-in Hi-Fi serves most rooms.

The house is closely linked with the outdoors, with terraces, courts or balconies off all rooms; a swimming pool and terrace is off the bedrooms. Room arrangement and fenestration is planned to give maximum privacy in spite of all the openness to the views.

Above left: the gallery linking service and living areas contains entry and dining area, gives big space for entertaining. Floors are blue-gray slate, exposed wood ceilings have a soft, "frosty" finish. The entrance court has a neat, small garden.

Left: the living room is quite big; half is shown here. Colors of fabrics and rugs repeat those of the stone. The room capitalizes on the views, yet gives feeling of security and enclosure. A grille and reception room below is reached by a dramatic stair.

GREAT STYLE ON A BUDGET

THE DECISION of knowing exactly what one wants in a house is often half the battle of achieving it. Mr. and Mrs. George Serulnic were quite definite in their ideas — a spacious contemporary hillside house with a really dramatic view — but their budget was very limited. Undaunted, they bought a seemingly impossible patch of hillside that had the view, and commissioned Richard J. Neutra, an architect well known for creating the kind of house they liked, to study their problem.

By extremely careful planning and budgeting, a house was created that completely delighted the clients. Fitted on a tiny site created out of the hillside, the small house is clean-cut, good looking — and seems enormous. Open, multi-purpose areas, glass walls to capitalize on the view, and simple structure and materials all add to this effect. There are even rather luxurious surprises: entrance court, bath with patio.

THE NEIGHBORHOOD: the house lies among scattered mountainside dwellings in La Cresenta, overlooking the Los Angeles area. There is a wonderful mountain panorama. During the day, different colored mountain slopes stretch as far as the eye can reach; at night, lights of the city glitter far below. On clear days, the ocean is visible. Other houses dotting the slopes are some distance away.

THE SITE: the architect states that when he visited the site for the first time, there seemed no possible way to get up — what he saw was simply several acres of precipitous slope. A small flat site for the house was cut out of the hillside, with a long winding road built to reach it.

Richard J. Neutra, Architect.
Fordyce S. Marsh, Contractor.

The plan of the Serulnic house is handled to give good area division, utmost sense of space. The entire glass wall slides open to add terrace to living area.
The sitting nook at right in photo below left converts for dining.
Entrance court (below center) has reflecting pool, lush plants

THE FAMILY: George and Dorothy Serulnic, a young couple, had their house planned while they were still engaged. Both work in the city. He is a musician, she a minister.

THE HOUSE: at the top of the winding drive, one reaches the parking area and carport. From there, one enters the house along the edge of the cut-out hillside through a small court with a shallow reflecting pool. On opening the door, one is faced with the wonderful panorama.

The open living area is bisected by a fireplace dividing the space into a family-guest room and the living room proper. A dining bay, near the kitchen, has a low table, patented by the architect, that can be raised to dining height when needed. Built-in furniture and storage walls are well planned to conserve space. The bathroom has a translucent wall over a sunken tub; one of the panes becomes a door opening into a lawn patio for sun bathing in full privacy. A planting scheme for enhancing house and privacy is being gradually developed.

THE ARCHITECT: Richard J. Neutra remarks, "How faith moves a mountain could be the motto for this small house perched on a mountain shelf gouged from the steep slope. The young couple knew what they wanted and they wanted it badly enough so that, in the long run, they overcame all obstacles. An excellent contractor overcame all the difficulties of the unusual site." Mr. Neutra also wished to note the efforts of his staff on this house: Dion Neutra, Benno Fischer, Serge Koschin, John Blanton, Toby Schmidbauer, Donald Polsky, Perry Neuschatz and Gunnar Serneblad.

OWNERS' REACTION: the architect notes that, "the owners receive a great deal of relaxation when leaving the hustle and bustle of human activity in the city below, and enjoy the peaceful landscape spread below them."

Perhaps the most dramatic view from the Serulnic house is at night (below). Note light strip in overhang to illuminate terrace. Glass walls slide into frame extending beyond house (left). The house has cement plaster finish outside, birch plywood and plaster inside. Floors are concrete

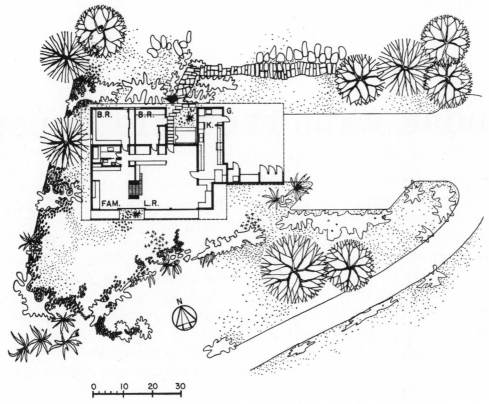

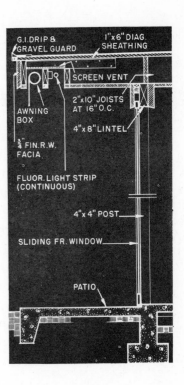

G.I. DRIP &
GRAVEL GUARD

1"x 6" DIAG.
SHEATHING

SCREEN VENT

2"x10" JOISTS
AT 16" O.C.

AWNING
BOX

4"x 8" LINTEL

¾" FIN. R.W.
FACIA

FLUOR. LIGHT STRIP
(CONTINUOUS)

4"x 4" POST

SLIDING FR. WINDOW

PATIO

0   10   20   30

B.R.   B.R.   G.

K.

FAM.   L.R.

N

KNORR-ELLIOTT ASSOCIATES,
DESIGNERS.
Mr. and Mrs. Robert Hilmer,
Owners.
Location: Atherton, California.
John E. Brown, Engineer.
Joseph Whelan Construction
Company, Contractor.

ERNEST BRAUN

ADOBE WALL PROTECTS HOUSE

The architectural trend toward introverted houses has already begun to penetrate the builder house field. This house, designed for a California builder, uses a blank adobe wall to mask its rich, congenial, inside world.

Because the house is located within the densely populated San Francisco Bay residential area, privacy was an important factor in the design. The blank wall façade isolates the lot and protects the two separate pavilions—one for sleeping, one for living and entertaining—which are set amid private gardens, a patio, and a reflecting pool. A steel frame structure frees the walls of any load-bearing obligations so that glass can be interchanged with adobe wherever light and views of the private outdoor areas are desired. An entry with glass walls and ceiling links the two pavilions and frames the reflecting pool which lies between them. Walls facing the patio are also glass.

The glass entrance (photo, right) leads past the reflecting pond and into the living room. A strip of glass between the roof and the north wall of the living area, glass panels on either side of the fireplace, and a wall of glass facing the patio admit natural light and intensify the impression of spaciousness.

The structure is particularly well expressed in the living area (photo, right bottom) where glass forms much of the curtain walls and the frame is left exposed. Shelves are hung from the steel studs.

A grill counter (photo below) separates the kitchen from the dining area, and serves as a pass-through and snack bar. A folding door which slides across the pass-through closes off the kitchen.

ERNEST BRAUN

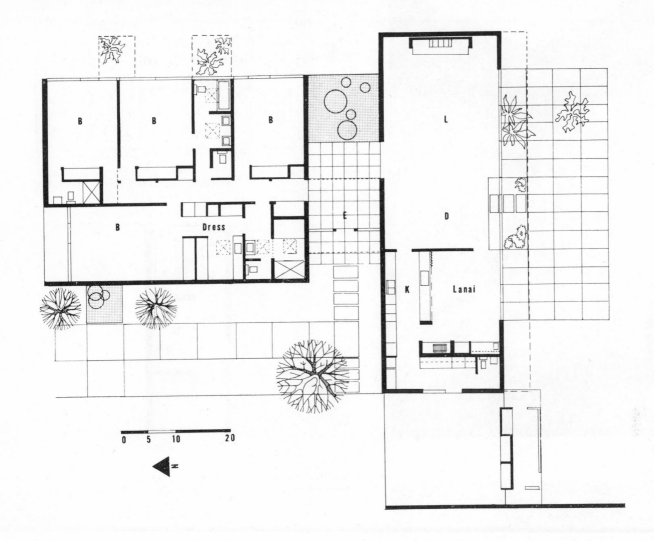

Pavilions Form Bi-Nuclear Plan . . .

MORLEY BAER

Functions of the two pavilions are clearly defined (see plan, above). Separation of the bedrooms from the living area serves to diminish noise and assure privacy in the sleeping area. The pavilions are constructed in simple, rectangular shapes which are least expensive to build. Ceiling heights vary from 8 ft in the bedroom wing to 10 ft in the living areas.

Skylights admit natural light to the bedrooms (see photo, left). Asphalt tile floors and ceilings of exposed 2 by 4 tongue-and-groove decking are easy to maintain. A single weathertight adobe wall forms the finish wall for both the interior and exterior.

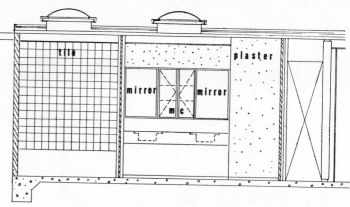

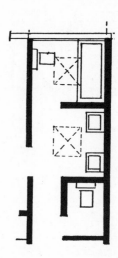

SECTION THROUGH CHILDREN'S BATH

The common bathroom which serves two of the children's bedrooms is partitioned into three areas (see plan above). Space for the water closet is almost totally enclosed but is nearest to the connecting passageway since it has the most traffic. Twin sinks allow simultaneous use of the dressing area (photo left) by both children.

A sunken tile tub adds luxury to the bathroom in the master suite (see photo left). Bathing and dressing areas are daylit by plastic bubble skylights (see plan, below) in both the master suite and the children's baths. Partitions separate the tub and shower stall, water closet, lavatory, and dressing area which is near wardrobe.

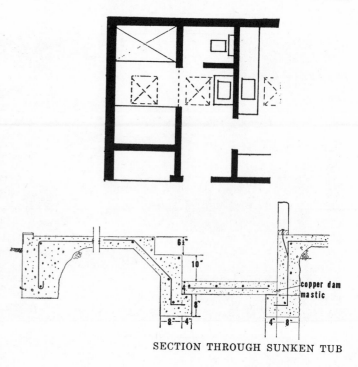

SECTION THROUGH SUNKEN TUB

PAUL HAYDEN KIRK, ARCHITECT. *Mr. and Mrs. Lewis J. Dowell, Owners. Location: Seattle, Washington. Stern & Towne, Mechanical Engineers. William G. Teufel, Landscape Architect.*

GARDENS INSIDE AND OUT

In addition to an extremely attractive and well organized exterior garden (above), this house also features a garden court completely closed from the weather (color plate VI). The court is used as a major theme for the design of the house: it affords a surprise vista on entering the house; it lends space and light to every major room in the house; and it doubles as extra living space and a luxurious stair well.

Perhaps it is worth considering here, that most all really good houses of the past or present have had some such dominant element (or series of elements) to seize the imagination. True, and fortunately, the exact forms and ideas have varied — some subtle, some startling, elaborate at times, often inexpensive. It may be that this is the most singular quality missing from our more humdrum houses. At the least, it helps remind one that, architecturally, houses need not be just a series of innocuous spaces to be "decorated" in the fashionable whim of the moment to give them a slight semblance of interest.

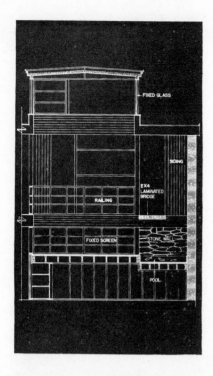

DEARBORN-MASSAR

The simple, textured stone front of the Lewis J. Dowell house makes a marked contrast with the open lightness of the interiors. The court is enclosed (because of the Seattle weather) by a glass penthouse which extends above the roof (photo above). The floor of the court is placed midway between the basement and main level. This gives the area sufficient height to make a strong focal point. It also makes an extremely pleasant transition level for the house, which is one story at the front, two at the back (note section).

Shoji screens make it possible to shut off areas from the court if desired (photo right). The rest of the house is also planned to give needed seclusion. The library-den is placed where it may be used with the living area for entertaining, or with the master bedroom to form a private apartment. A balcony and stairs link this suite with the outside garden. The children's rooms are on the lower level, and also form a separate suite with a workshop and indoor and outdoor play areas.

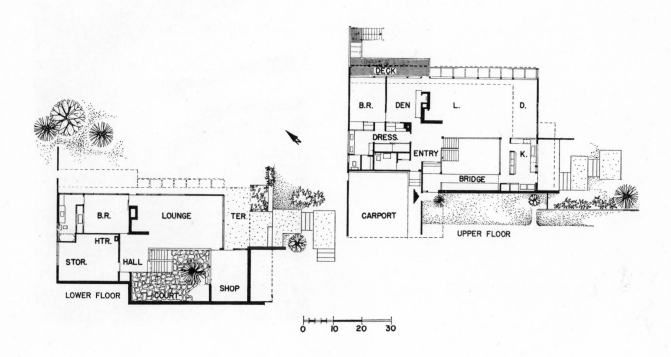

As Mrs. Dowell had spent a good part of her life in the Orient, the design and materials of the house have slight Eastern overtones to form an appropriate background for collections and mementos, contemporary furnishings.

The structure is framed in Douglas fir and steel, and exterior walls are Oregon basalt stone or Western red cedar. The roofing is built-up, surfaced with white marble chips.

Interior walls are walnut veneer or hemlock. The den and master bedroom were carefully sized to fit two Oriental carpets exactly.

CASUAL EASE FOR FAMILY LIFE

A very personal and controlling attitude of the clients dominated the design of this house. They hold a strong belief that a house belongs to the whole family, and that all main living areas — insofar as practicable — be open to the children and their friends. This is in direct contrast to the current trend in many contemporary houses, where emphasis is on increasing separation between the activities of the different age groups. An extremely pleasant, easy-going house is the successful result.

The family of five is headed by a busy doctor and his wife; she is exceptionally interested in civic and community affairs. The children include a boy age 10, and two girls ages 8 and 6. To assure freedom of living for all in a house providing generous and casual living space inside and out, simplicity and ease of housekeeping was carefully provided for. Each room has quick, direct access to the terraces which surround the house. The site has no particular view, but boasts a fine grove of trees, privacy from neighbors.

MALONE AND HOOPER, ARCHITECTS. *Dr. and Mrs. Russell R. Klein, Owners. Location: Kentfield, California. Wilson & Wedekind, Contractors. Buonaccorsi & Murray, Mechanical Engineers. Lawrence Halprin, Landscape Architect.*

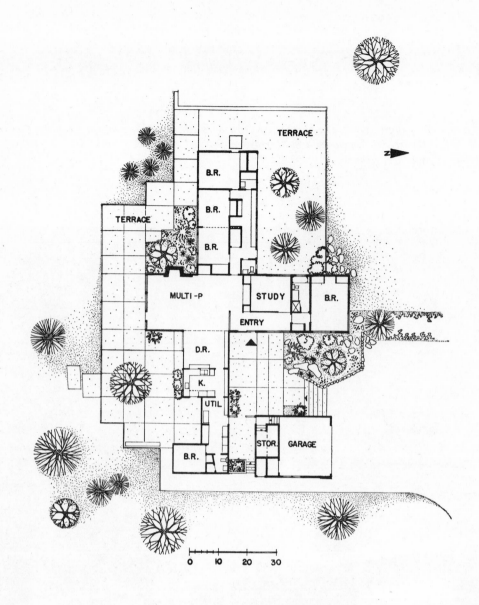

ERNEST BRAUN

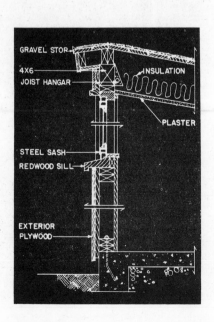

The main area of the Russell R. Klein house combines living and dining space into a single multi-use space (photo above). The room is large enough to absorb the activities of all the members of the family: snacks at the bar counter, games at the dining table, block play on the floor, televiewing, and adult conversation around the fireplace. Changes in ceiling height and clerestory windows add interest and brightness to the room.

Other elements of the house are grouped in wings around this central room. The master bedroom flanks a study to form a suite for the parents. Children's bedrooms are in a wing of their own; their bathroom is split to minimize congestion, and the corridor between provides generous toy storage under the windows. Sliding panels permit the girls' rooms to be joined into a single area. The service areas are at the other end of the house, and include a children's entrance with a large coat and boot closet and adjacent bath. This entrance opens off the same front court as the formal entry (photo left).

IDEAL FOR COUNTRY LIVING

The effectiveness of natural simplicity in the proper setting is highly apparent in this house. It is unpretentious and casual in plan and design, without much regard for rules set by formalities of more suburban areas. Yet the house is lifted high above the ordinary by a bold and positive character that seems to belong just where it is.

The site consists of some six acres of sloping land, including a small promontory which made a natural building location. Here, the house overlooks the town of Healdsburg in the valley, the winding Russian River, and timbered hills beyond. To make the most of this view, the side of the house facing it is almost completely glazed. Exterior match-stick blinds are hung from these westerly eaves in summer to cut sky glare. In the dining area (right) an angled window was designed to exploit the complete sweep of the panorama.

To minimize grading and preserve the large oak that umbrellas over the house, the plan is on two levels; living areas step up with the slope from dining and work areas.

MARIO CORBETT, ARCHITECT. *Mr. and Mrs. Leo Frediani, owners. Location: Healdsburg, California. Leo Frediani, Contractor.*

The house amply fulfills the owners' requirements. It was to be specifically designed for country living — open, informal, and easy to maintain. A sleeping area was to be provided for an unmarried son, and separate guest quarters for visitors or other family members. Access to the outdoors was to be freely provided for each room.

To obtain the maximum freedom and living area in the plan, sliding walls are used between work and dining areas, and between living room and bedrooms. Thus the entire house can become a single large room for various occasions.

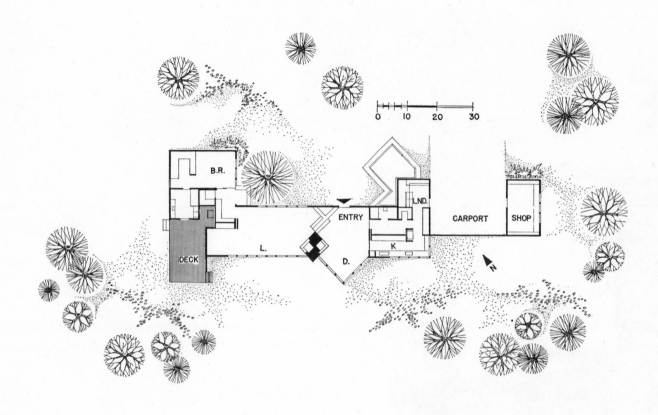

STONE AND STECCATI

Finishes in the Leo Frediani house also reflect its informal, easy-to-keep qualities. Most walls, inside and out, are natural redwood; a few are grass cloth over plasterboard. Clear fir planks and beams are left exposed for the ceilings. All floors are cork except in the dining area, where cement topping is dyed and waxed in variegated shades of brown.

These materials are also used in the master bathroom (above center), where even the tub is made of redwood ply. This bath connects to a sundeck and a future swimming pool.

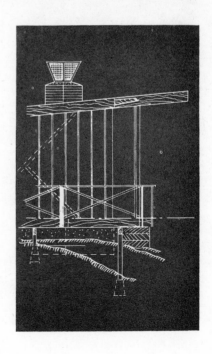

GOOD TEAMWORK, GOOD HOUSE

Cᴏɴᴛʀᴀʀʏ to certain popular fiction about hazardous architect-owner relations during the building of a house, the experience is usually an important, exciting, and very pleasant one. This house for Mr. and Mrs. James Kelso, in Kentfield, California, is an excellent case in point. Understanding and cooperation were as serene and competent as the resulting house. And the unaffected, easy simplicity of the design is certainly all the better for the accord. Strangers at the outset, the owners and architect have developed a high mutual esteem through their joint efforts in the project. Their pertinent comments on the planning and building of the house are quoted below.

Tʜᴇ Nᴇɪɢʜʙᴏʀʜᴏᴏᴅ: the house is in Kent Woodlands, a beautifully tended section in Marin County, just north of the Golden Gate Bridge. Wooded hills look down toward the bay in the distance, and around at the hills of Marin. All building and landscaping in the area must have plans submitted to an architectural supervising committee for approval. However, there are no set restrictions, other than a general understanding that white flat roofs will not be acceptable — due to reflective glare when seen from homes at a higher level on the hills.

Tʜᴇ Sɪᴛᴇ: moderately large in size, the wooded lot slopes gently down from the road. But for all intents, the house rests on level land. The cumulative drop was utilized behind the house to place a guest house and pool as low as possible on the site so they would not dominate the outlook or obscure the view from the main rooms.

Wurster, Bernardi and Emmons, Architects. Wilson and Wedekind, Contractor. Duncan Monro, Landscape Architect.

Textured patterns of the landscaping point up the simple natural quality of the house. Main rooms at the rear are extended by broad covered and open terraces, and pool and guesthouse beyond

THE FAMILY: requirements were relatively simple — three children and the parents needed space for the usual activities, and adequate separation (because of age differences) between the quarters of the daughter and those of the two younger brothers.

THE HOUSE: sensitive handling of natural materials and finishes quietly blend the house and landscaping into its suburban setting. The paving and arrangement of the entrance approach are especially worthy of note.

The plan was arranged with living areas in the center, flanked by rooms for the boys (with an outdoor exit) on one side, quarters for the parents and daughter on the other. Banks of closets and baths zone bedrooms for quiet. The monitor for daylight over interior dressing rooms, bath, and hall was carefully detailed to avoid the heavy look that so often spoils this kind of element. Hot water radiant heating is used.

THE ARCHITECTS: Donn Emmons, of Wurster, Bernardi and Emmons, handled the job for the firm, and reports: "The Kelsos were ideal clients and sympathetic and pleasant to work with. It was a happy and uncomplicated job, with no really unusual or difficult problems. The usual ones were, of course, present — budget, determination of what the living patterns should be, the somewhat restricted (for the area) size of the lot."

OWNERS' REACTION: "The planning and building was an enjoyable experience. We did not know Mr. Emmons prior to planning our home, but after our first meeting he understood our requirements and ideas. We were sorry when it was over! But everything has worked out perfectly. The arrangement of the rooms is ideal for us. The house is very easy to keep and requires very little outside help. And all our landscaping requires only a half a day a week gardening service."

The Kelsos wanted a positive difference of character in the living and family rooms. This led to the use of teak in entry and living room, California cedar in family room (below). Guest house and pool are as neatly designed and detailed as the main house

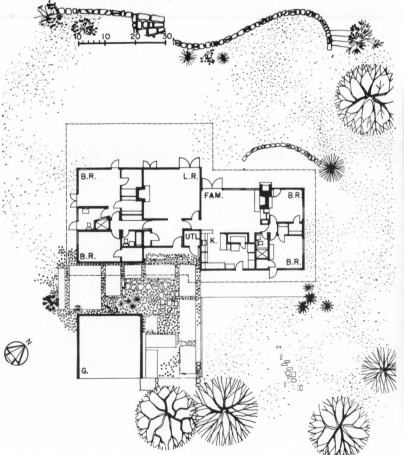

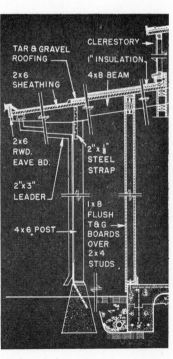

TAR & GRAVEL
ROOFING

CLERESTORY

1" INSULATION

2x6
SHEATHING

4x8 BEAM

2x6
RWD.
EAVE BD.

2"x ⅛"
STEEL
STRAP

2"x3"
LEADER

1x8
FLUSH
T&G
BOARDS
OVER
2x4
STUDS

4x6 POST

WURSTER, BERNARDI AND EMMONS | 181

W. FRAZIER OVERPECK, ARCHITECT. *Mr. and Mrs. Peter Gowland, Owners. Location: Santa Monica, California. Paul Greenfield, Structural Engineer.*

MULTI-USE ROOM EXPANDS HOUSE

This clean, crisp house offers a very interesting plan arrangement for those who pursue careers or serious hobbies at home. The owners are a photographer-illustrator team, and the house includes complete facilities for their work: studio, darkroom, office, dressing room and bath for models, and a workshop for constructing sets and props. Though this wing can be closed-off from the rest of the house for work, at other periods it augments the living areas in a variety of ways.

Plastic panels open the studio to the living area for added living and entertainment or recreation space. The office becomes a family study, the bath a powder room. On special occasions, the entire wing could be converted into a private suite for grandparents or guests. This multi-use wing gives the house the conveniences of a much larger establishment. The close relationship of indoor and outdoor areas in the house further increases useful space and provides a pleasant setting for the casual Southern California life.

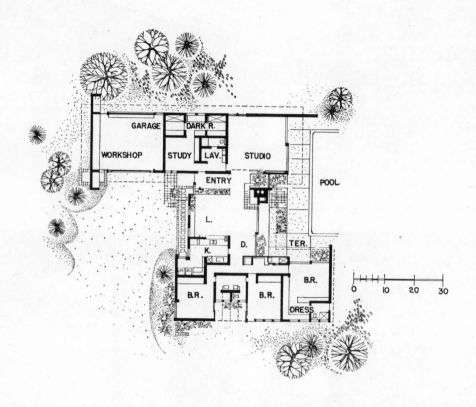

The living room of the Peter Gowland house is itself conceived as a "multi-purpose," "family room" kind of area. Terrazzo floors and other easy-to-keep surfaces make it practical as a children's playroom as well as an area for general living and dining. The kitchen opens directly into the living area via a bar-height counter and offers good visual control of play areas and pool.

Each bedroom has an outside entrance to reduce tracking from the pool and excess traffic through the living area. The children's rooms open onto a private court, and are joined by a compartmentalized bath.

Most all rooms have sliding glass walls opening onto terraces. Planting areas are carried through the house to help visually link these areas. To extend the season for outdoor living, radiant heating is installed in terraces and in garage work areas as well as in all interior floors.

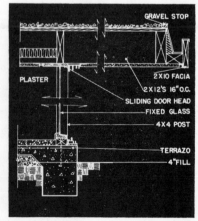

Plate VII

OVERPECK

INDOOR-OUTDOOR PRIVACY

O UTDOOR LIVING AREAS, closely related to indoor spaces, are perhaps as vital to Californians (and many others of us) as the more traditional roof-over-head. But in the more highly populated areas, extremely careful planning is necessary to prevent a fishbowl existence within such a house. For his own home in Pacific Palisades, California, Architect Frederick E. Emmons has worked out a very practical scheme of opening all rooms onto a series of delightful inner courts and gardens. Blank walls and fences (and one small window) face street and neighbors. The lushness of the setting, and careful use of several materials — redwood and plaster siding, concrete block and translucent glass fences — prevent any sense of bleakness from lack of windows on the façade.

THE NEIGHBORHOOD: in this proverbial Land of the Automobile, fairly heavy traffic could be expected around the corner lot selected. This, of course, increased the need for privacy. It was also desired to have attractive approaches to the house from either street for the convenience of guests and family.

THE SITE: nine very large, closely spaced oak trees added both glamor and interest to the relatively small, gently sloping plot. In order to save as many as possible, considerable time had to be spent in accurately measuring distances and heights of projecting limbs in order to squeeze the plan in and around the trees. Only the two least desirable trees were finally sacrificed; and the house actually comes within an inch of three of the remaining ones.

A. Quincy Jones & Frederick E. Emmons, Architects. Pat Hamilton, Contractor. Eckbo, Royston & Williams, Landscape Architects.

1957 Award of Merit, National AIA Award Program

Considerable esthetic appeal results from tree-saving efforts in this house. Slight changes in levels, heights, wall projections, to avoid roots and limbs add needed interest to windowless façades

JULIUS SHULMAN

THE FAMILY: Mr. and Mrs. Emmons and their teenage daughter desired to have a house with as much area as possible for family living and informal entertaining. Thus every attempt was to be made to open the living area into the outdoor spaces under the magnificent trees.

THE HOUSE: A near-Oriental concept of a house compound very successfully solves the needs for routine living and the family's special interests. Three pavilions — for living, sleeping, and garage-storage — are connected by covered or glassed-in loggias, and are placed to create a series of individual gardens. Each garden has at least one of the trees, and becomes an extension of an indoor room or a private room to itself. The carport is at a lower level than the rest of the house, screened by a block retaining wall. Its connecting passage forms an attractive secondary entrance. An uncovered service and kitchen entrance is also from this side. The study can double as a guest room.

With the lack of a sun problem (due to the trees), all glass wall areas were carried up to the ceilings to allow views of the overhanging branches. This condition also allows a plastic skylight in the bath without discomfort. Construction is relatively simple: wood stud frame with plaster and redwood siding, concrete slab floor with radiant heating, concrete block walls and chimney. The same materials are used for interior finishes, plus burlap for a living room wall and cork or plastic tile for floors. Gardens are paved in a variety of surfacings.

OWNERS' (AND ARCHITECTS') REACTION: "Despite the small size of the lot, complete privacy is obtained. It might be added that the feeling of space is heightened by the fact that by opening the living room on both sides, one can see the entire usable area of the lot from all terraces."

The Frederick Emmons house shows well how attractive fences and screens can be used in an architectural way to give privacy, extend vista from within. Right and below left: the central courtyard. Below: living room opens both sides to gardens. The plan is laid out with a thoughtful eye to convenient circulation

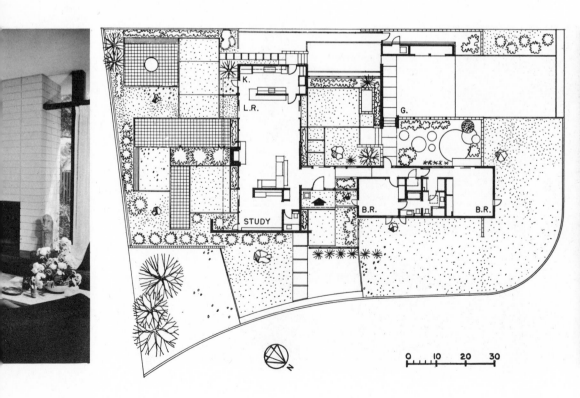

K.

L.R.

G.

STUDY

B.R.

B.R.

N

0   10   20   30

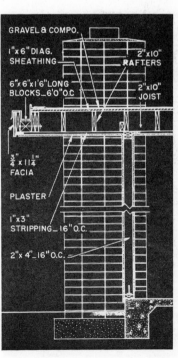

GRAVEL & COMPO.

1"x6" DIAG.
SHEATHING

2"x10"
RAFTERS

6"x6"x1'6"LONG
BLOCKS 6'0"O.C.

2"x10"
JOIST

3/4 x 11¼"
FACIA

PLASTER

1"x3"
STRIPPING 16" O.C.

2"x 4' 16"O.C.

These photographs of the study in the Emmons house give a clear example of flexible indoor-outdoor relationships. Baffle walls (and curtains) give adequate privacy for homework or occasional guest room use. Yet the area opens directly to living room and terrace to add entertaining space

KILLINGSWORTH, BRADY AND SMITH, ARCHITECTS.

Mr. and Mrs. Richard Opdahl, Owners.

Location: Long Beach, California.

Alfred P. Dorsey, Contractor.

John Nicholson of Frank Brothers, Interior Designer.

A SMALL LOT WELL USED

Here is a deft solution to the design challenge presented by the shrinking availability and size of house lots in our burgeoning urban centers. This town house was designed for a 30- by 80-ft lot bordered by a two-story apartment building on one side, and a one-and-one-half-story house on the other. Given those restrictions, the architects met the family's needs for space and privacy while creating a house rich in delightful visual experiences.

Separation from the neighboring buildings was achieved by setting two 18-ft high walls 3 ft from the side yard lines. The house is developed within these walls, and is enclosed at both ends by glass panels. A modified post and beam structural system was used to accommodate the open plan of the house and the limited width of the property. The living area, with its glass façade, is set back 41 ft from the property line on the street side to make room for a carport, entrance garden, patio and reflecting pool.

Walled Garden Isolates a City Site . . .

Precast concrete stepping stones lead from the street through an entrance garden to a 6-ft high wrought iron fence. Beyond the fence, the steps—which are anchored in a concrete base—seem to float on the 21- by 24-ft reflecting pool (see photo above). A patio of concrete slabs also rests on the pool. Since the side walls of the house extend beyond the pool (see plan, opposite page), the lush patio-pool area is isolated from neighboring buildings. A circulating pump keeps the pool at a 6-in. level.

Kitchen cabinets and counters are designed to look like furniture (see photo right). Delicate, ⅝-in. iron legs raise the cabinets 1 ft from the floor. A self-edged, plastic laminated top protects the woodwork from burning, cutting, and spilled liquids. Sink, burners, and disposal are built into the cabinets. Kitchen and bathroom floors are vinyl asbestos, walls are plaster.

A gently curved staircase with open treads and wrought iron handrail (see photo far right) serves the second floor bedroom-bathroom area. Though the staircase can be seen from the entrance (photo above), it is situated at the rear of the house near a glass wall which overlooks a private garden. The bedroom level terminates in a balcony over the two-story living room. Side walls (photo, far right) are redwood stained an eucalyptus gold which sets the color tone for the house: white, orange, and yellow.

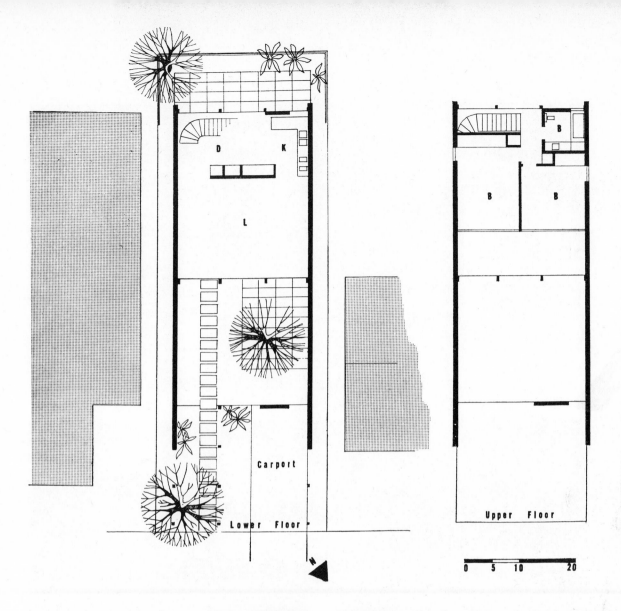

Carport

Lower Floor

Upper Floor

0 5 10   20

A HOUSE AROUND AN ATRIUM

The introverted, closed-front house, often associated with more crisp and formal design, has adopted here the relaxed and casual mood of the familiar Northwest house. Built of rugged, natural materials with durable surfaces, the house is particularly well adapted to family living.

The plan is arranged in the shape of a hollow U with an atrium, or entrance court, located in the core. Because the house is situated at the top of a 300-ft-high conical hill and is comparatively isolated, much use is made of sliding glass doors and full length glass panels in the rear exterior walls. Thus, inside rooms look onto the pleasant atrium and outside rooms afford long views to the Rogue River Valley. The kitchen, den, and family room are grouped together for easy coordination of family activities. Bedrooms are located in the east wing—away from noise—and are exposed to morning sun.

GEORGE T. ROCKRISE, ARCHITECT.
Mr. and Mrs. Dunbar Carpenter, Owners.
Location: Medford, Oregon.
William B. Gilbert, Structural Engineer.
Buonacorsi and Murray, Mechanical Engineers.
Lawrence Halprin, Landscape Architect.
Dunbar Carpenter, Contractor.

1959 Award of Merit, National AIA Award Program

ERNEST BRAUN

Lightly scaled wood pillars, spaced at regular intervals, form the colonnades and covered walkways that encircle the house. Though there is a side door through which direct connection can be made from the carport to the family room and food storage area, the carport has been brought to the front of the house so that entrance can be made easily through the atrium. A covered walkway and loggia provide a protected access to the front door. The use of pebbles, trees, fountains, and concrete surfaces in the atrium has produced a pleasant garden atmosphere and requires little upkeep. The atrium, plus a deep porch and terrace to the north, afford varied outdoor dining and lounging areas.

A built-in cabinet in the family room serves as a room divider, pass-through from laundry, bookcase, and writing desk. On the laundry side it provides storage and working space. Floors are concrete slab on grade with a colored cement topping (photo right).

Vertical white cedar walls contrast with a native fieldstone fireplace in the living area. The ceiling is composed of 2- by 6-in. tongue-and-groove decking over 4- by 4-in. exposed beams. Sliding glass doors and panels open onto both the atrium and the porch (center right).

The use of native fieldstone and natural wood lend a different quality to the bathroom. A skylight admits natural light to the mirror and dressing area. Translucent sliding glass panels separate the sunken tile tub from a private terrace. The sink is built-in with a cabinet beneath for storing towels and other linens (far right).

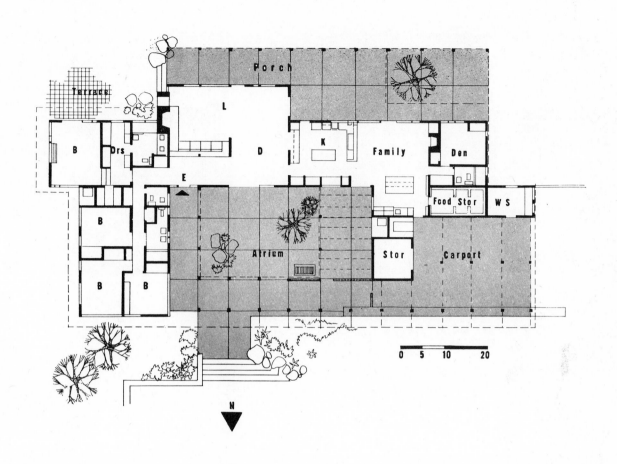

Porch

Terrace

L

B   Drs

D   K   Family   Den

E

Food Stor   W S

B   Atrium   Stor   Carport

B   B

0   5   10   20

N

ERNEST BRAUN

A. QUINCY JONES & FREDERICK E. EMMONS, ARCHITECTS. *Eichler Homes, Builder. Location: San Mateo, California. William R. Mason, Structural Design. Douglas Baylis, Landscape Architect. Anne K. Knorr, Interior Design*

STEEL FRAME FLEXIBLE PLAN

A new sense of undisturbed space and freedom to move about evolves from the particularly flexible plan of this house. The structural steel framework is engineered to make load-bearing walls unnecessary, thus freeing the interiors from restricting, floor to ceiling barriers. Rooms flow into one another, changing character gradually with the help of shifting moods in color. Glass walls integrate garden with interiors.

Essentially an experimental house, the X-100 was designed for Eichler Homes to test new construction materials and to project planning ideas which seem to suit new living patterns — informal but gracious with much emphasis on close indoor-outdoor relationship. All rooms are located along the perimeter where they can utilize outdoor space. Sliding glass doors lead from the children's bedroom to a play yard at the front of the house enclosed by a concrete block wall (photo above). Some of the blocks are reversed to give a pierced effect and to allow light.

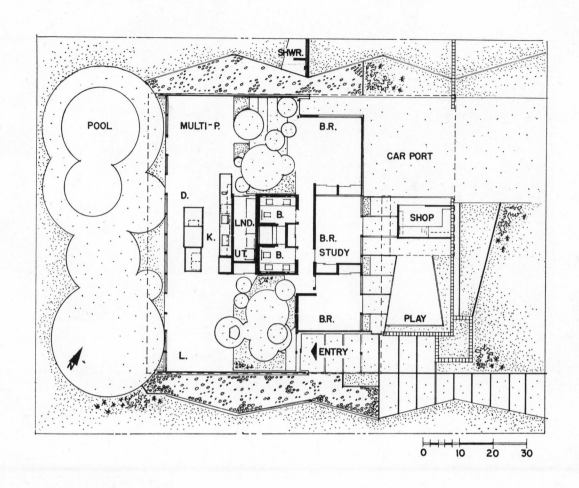

POOL

MULTI-P.

SHWR.

B.R.

CAR PORT

D.

LND.

B.

SHOP

K.

B.R.
STUDY

UT.

B.

B.R.

PLAY

L.

ENTRY

0   10   20   30

ERNEST BRAUN

ERNEST BRAUN

The X-100 employs high-density overlay fir panels along the bedroom wall. Indoors, the bedrooms are enclosed by draperies. Kitchen and dining area are also separated by sliding drapery partitions. The interiors can thus be closed off for privacy or opened completely from east to west wall. Exposed steel beams, painted cinnamon red, run across the ceiling. Roof panels are interrupted by a 32-ft skylight to provide natural lighting. A kitchen, two baths, utility area and laundry room are grouped in a central core, which saves stringing expensive plumbing lines to separate areas.

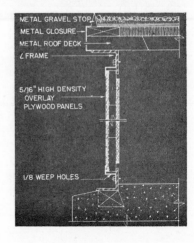

METAL GRAVEL STOP
METAL CLOSURE
METAL ROOF DECK
∠ FRAME

5/16" HIGH DENSITY
OVERLAY
PLYWOOD PANELS

1/8 WEEP HOLES

Plate VIII   JONES & EMMONS

COLONNADES DISTINGUISH HOME

THE DECORATIVE QUALITY of exposed structural elements has been made a very dramatic feature in this San Rafael, California, house. With no trace of quaintness or gaudiness, natural materials and a simple, modular post and beam structure give the house an exuberant vitality. The long ranges of free-standing posts form colonnades for divisions between galleries and living areas. For all the openness, individual areas still retain an amazing degree of privacy.

Architects Anshen and Allen were commissioned by Builder Herbert A. Crocker to design a distinctive home, and include all appliances, a $12,000 lot, landscaping, and architects' fees, to be sold at a pre-determined price of $39,500. This spacious, economical design is the result.

THE NEIGHBORHOOD: the house is located in the Green Valley Country Club Tract, on the outskirts of San Rafael, California. It is a residential development, with generous lots bordering on a golf course. The area is surrounded by the wooded Solano and Napa County hills.

THE SITE: there is an acre of land, flat near the street. This area was used as the actual building site. Behind the house, the land rolls up to a tree-covered hill crest. The street lies to the north of the plot.

THE FAMILY: this house had the unusual circumstance of satisfying two "clients" — the builder, Mr. Crocker, as the primary client, and Dr. Arons, who bought it, as the ultimate one. As such, it had to reflect the needs of a typical-sized family in the best possible way.

Anshen and Allen, Architects.
Robert O. Dewell, Engineer.
Herbert A. Crocker & Co.,
Developer and General Contractor.

The economical device of using exposed construction for architectural effect gives this house unusual distinction. High windows in the redwood front give privacy from the street, while the back is open wide to terrace

THE HOUSE: the open planning, and the gable roof of exposed post and beam construction, provide a fine sense of spaciousness in the house. Variation in the roof height helps suggest room separations, and gives low hanging eaves for sun protection. Openings in the roof over entry and terrace help daylight living areas. All major rooms open onto the terrace, and together, form an immense area for entertaining. An all purpose family room adjoins the kitchen, and is used for regular meals and lounging. The small living room is used for formal dining. An attic room is over the garage, which has space for a workshop.

THE ARCHITECTS: Anshen and Allen note that, "Our actual client for this house was the builder, and the problem that of designing a spacious, attractive house, to be sold at a modest price. Architecturally, the solution required the development of a simple overall form and structural system, with all architectural interest being created within this economical framework."

BUILDERS REACTION: Herbert A. Crocker responds, "Through the courtesy of the Arons, we were able to show the house to the public. Customers were impressed with the unique but practical design of the home, and in most cases 'appraised' the value of the package at $10–15,000 over the actual price. We feel that this result was achieved through a happy combination of builder and architect's talent and experience."

OWNER'S REACTION: Dr. and Mrs. J. Arons state, "We visited the house when it was only halfway completed. We fell in love with the location, the lot, the plan of the house and the wonderful feeling of great spaciousness that such an open plan seems to create. Since we moved into the house, we have found every moment a delightful experience."

A simple roof, with no jogs, covers the entire house. Most hallways are eliminated by the open gallery. The multi-purpose room (below, center) has its own bath. Interiors are mahogany, redwood, fir ceilings. Heating is by a two-zoned perimeter system

ROGER STURTEVANT

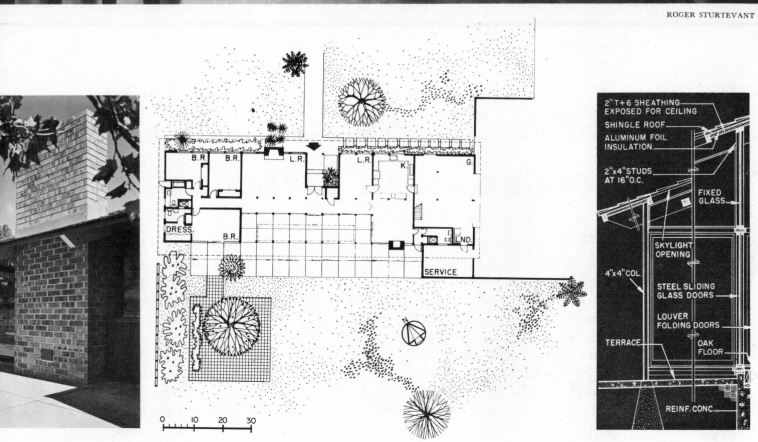

B.R. B.R. L.R. L.R. K. G.

DRESS.

B.R.

SERVICE

0 10 20 30

2" T+6 SHEATHING
EXPOSED FOR CEILING
SHINGLE ROOF
ALUMINUM FOIL
INSULATION

2"x4" STUDS
AT 16" O.C.

FIXED
GLASS

SKYLIGHT
OPENING

4"x4" COL.

STEEL SLIDING
GLASS DOORS

LOUVER
FOLDING DOORS

TERRACE

OAK
FLOOR

REINF. CONC.

ORDER ON AN IRREGULAR SITE

Much of the order and the amenities associated with costlier housing have been incorporated in the design of this strictly budgeted, easy to maintain house. An irregular site (such sites are frequently found at lower costs than flat, "perfect" sites) has been utilized in this case to gain an integral carport, to minimize excavation, and to provide a view in three directions. Only the entrance court to the west required landscaping, since the other sides of the house face or extend into natural wooded areas. The court itself is a privacy factor: an L-shaped fence of vertical wood posts sets off the court and obstructs the view from the street.

Planned and built in two stages, the house is an excellent example of how initial construction can be kept within a budget, and more space added logically later on. The new wing provides a master suite and utility room.

WILLIAM L. FLETCHER, ARCHITECT AND OWNER.

Location: Portland, Oregon.
H. L. Wooley, Mechanical Engineer.
Fred McCarroll, Contractor (original construction).
Ellis-Andrews, Contractors (addition).

Materials and Plan Produce Commodious Quality . . .

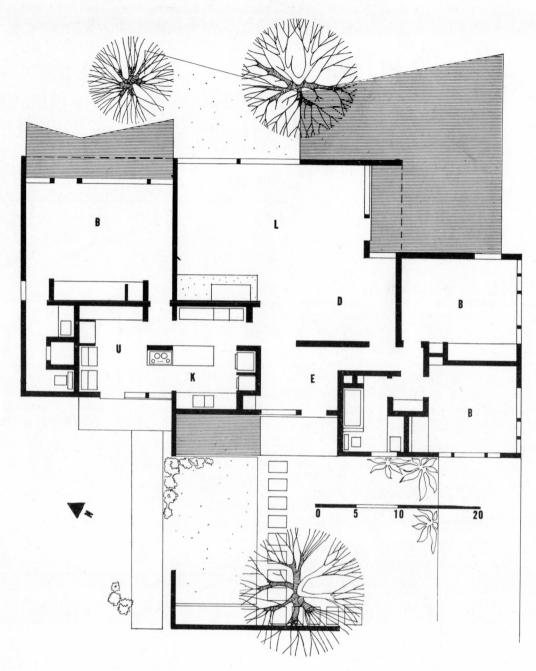

Materials used are natural and serviceable. The entrance court is formed of native plants (pines, ferns, etc.) together with gravel, rocks, and concrete paving. Exterior walls of the house are resawn cedar tongue-and-groove siding on 2 by 4 studs.

The wood frame structure, crisp and orderly, is painted white wherever exposed. Interior partitions are hemlock panels over 2 by 4 studs. Floors are cork tile in living areas.

The commodious quality of this house is stressed in the planning and in the use of materials, such as in the living room (photo right). Laminated fir strips form the walls and ceiling. Foundation for the fireplace is stone in cement; the metal hood was specially fabricated. High, narrow windows on the street side give way to full-length glass panels where the house faces secluded woods. (photo below). Circulation is achieved with a minimum of space devoted to hallways (see plan at left). Two wood decks project out into shade trees.

TOM BURNS, JR.

The island counter (photo above) is equipped with pull-out trays for napkins and placemats, slots for storing knives along the chopping surface, and drawers for utensils, pans.

All cabinets are walnut with white plastic laminate counter surfaces. Sliding doors on the upper cabinets are painted white (photo right). Floor is surfaced with 3/16-in cork tile.

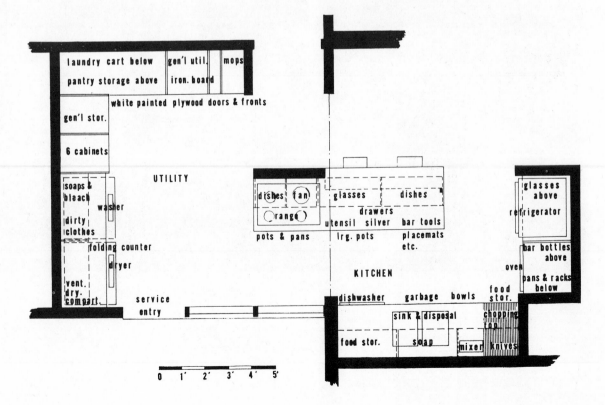

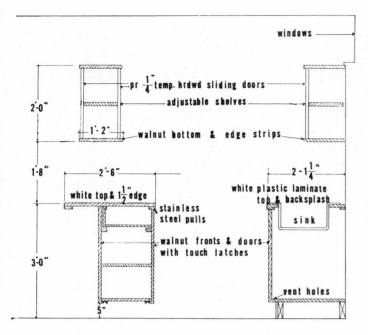

windows

pr ¼" temp. hrdwd sliding doors

adjustable shelves

2'-0"

1'-2"

walnut bottom & edge strips

1'-8"

2'-6"

2-1¼"

white top & 1½" edge

white plastic laminate top & backsplash

stainless steel pulls

sink

walnut fronts & doors with touch latches

3'-0"

vent holes

5"

A unified **arrangement** of kitchen, laundry, and utility room was developed in this house to cut down the housewife's work load by saving steps, and to capitalize on available space. The kitchen and laundry were so well related in the original structure that only a minimum amount of readjusting was necessary in order to integrate the utility room when the new wing was added (broken line in plan at bottom left marks the end of original structure). The utility room provides space for ironing, for general storage, and for extra equipment (drip drying cabinets, ventilated mop closets, etc.) Washing and drying machines were moved from the counter where the 21- by 31-in. double sink and dishwasher are now located (and where plumbing was already available) to the north wall of the utility room. The island counter was then transformed into an eating bar and work counter with a cooking top. Separate access to the eating bar from the utility room, the master suite, and the living-dining areas keeps traffic out of the kitchen proper. The oven is near the dining area so foods can be served hot.

Plan Unites Kitchen, Utility, Laundry Equipment . . .

TOM BURNS, JR.

DESIGN SOLVES SITE PROBLEM

Smith and Williams, Architects.
William C. Crowell Co., Contractor.
Eckbo, Roylston & Williams, Landscape Architects.

The street side of the house has intimate, compact scale, and strong Japanese character. Walk sheltered by wide overhang leads from garage and motor court, past sunken garden, to main entrance

IN MOST GOOD NEIGHBORHOODS, there is at least one solitary plot lying fallow and dispirited because, due to some topographical quirk, it has been considered too difficult or expensive to build on. Grading, filling or complex foundations *can* cost a lot, and as a result, relatively flat open land is generally sought-after for economical houses. But, in spite of the cliffs, ravines, or what have you, that mark these neglected tracts, they may have more scenic beauty — and are usually considerably lower in cost than adjoining sites.

Without resorting to any extreme eccentricities of structure or design, the architects of this house for Mr. and Mrs. Robert Crowell, in Pasadena, California, have devised a very good one-story answer for such a problem site. The house also harbors a number of planning ideas for any type of plot. Worth particular note is its Japanese aura; whether consciously striven for or not, it is becoming a significant trend, perhaps because of its blending of modesty with great style.

THE NEIGHBORHOOD: tracts in the area carry restrictions requiring a minimum house size of 3500 square feet, or four family bedrooms, and resistance to earthquakes. Pasadena, of course, is balmy, tree-studded, rolling, and its people delight in informal outdoor living.

THE SITE: peculiarities of this lot include a very steep slope, and a large amount of filled ground on the flat area near the street. The slope is heavily wooded, offering a nearly idyllic privacy, and it overlooks a meandering creek at its base.

JULIUS SHULMAN

THE FAMILY: the Crowells and their teen-age son required a one floor house with a large living room, four bedrooms (one would serve for guests, study or a maid), and a family TV room with a flexible partition opening on living or dining room. They dislike fussy ornament.

THE HOUSE: to adjust to the site condition, the house proper was constructed on flat filled ground near the street. Caissons were employed for grade beams, using existing grade and forms (no expensive special wood forms were needed). Extra living space was gained outdoors by building a deck of lighter, less expensive construction out over the slope.

The structure is economical, has great clarity; a modular system of posts and beams at four-foot intervals is used throughout. All walls not required to resist horizontal sheer for earthquake loads were eliminated. The remaining spaces between posts are filled with glass panes or louvers. Panels are clear, translucent or opaque — depending on outlook and exposure. The plan is well organized, circulation good; family bedroom wing can be shut-off, guests are apart, living spaces join together.

THE ARCHITECTS: Smith and Williams felt that the "problem of an uneven site in relationship to the level of the floor would be best expressed architecturally by a clear delineation of the floor line. We cantilevered house walls one foot beyond the grade beam and ran a continuous sill around the building. The result: shadow and sharp emphasis of the line."

OWNERS' REACTION: "*Very* favorable," say the Crowells. "The house takes full advantage of the best outlook and protects privacy; closeness to the outdoors is quite relaxing. Everything is convenient, comfortable and easy to care for. We like the simplicity and straight lines, the soft look and variation in color and grain of the stained redwood."

The back of the Crowell house seems vast, open, with deck extending living area into tree tops. Exterior rolling slat blinds and overhangs shield glass walls from sun; stained glass panes give interesting accents. Section (right) shows simplicity of structure. Landscaping deftly echoes the the character of the house

JULIUS SHULMAN

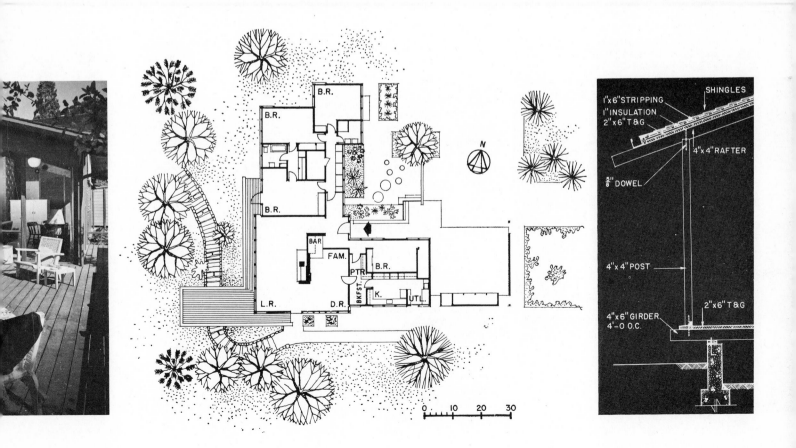

BAR

FAM.

PTR.

B.R.

B.R.

B.R.

B.R.

L.R.

D.R.

BKFST.

K.

UTL.

N

0   10   20   30

SHINGLES

1"x6"STRIPPING
1"INSULATION
2"x6"T&G

4"x4"RAFTER

5/8"DOWEL

4"x4"POST

2"x6"T&G

4"x6"GIRDER
4'-0 O.C.

INDEX

Pedersen, Arnold, 87
Pekruhn, John, 34-37
Phalen, Stanley I., 26
Phoenixville, Pa.; Webb house, 39-43
Pickett, Harold, Monostructure, 143
Pickman, Mr. and Mrs. David, 26-29
Platform; house on, 68, 130
Pool; reflecting, 85, 162-164, 192
   swimming, 82-83, 178, 184
Porch, screened, 126, 138
   see also; Court; Terrace
Portland, Ore.; Fletcher house, 204-
   209
Prefabrication, 143
Prize-winning houses; *see* Award-
   winning houses

R

Raleigh, N.C.; Matsumoto house, 151-
   153
Raybeck, Inc., 10
Redington Beach, Fla.; Nims house,
   127
Reflecting pool; *see* Pool
Rockrise, George T., 194-197
Rockwell, Mr. and Mrs. H. P. Davis,
   80-83
Rogers, D. S., 136
Roof; arches for, 110
   construction of, 54, 143
   sloping, 130-131
   see also Construction; Walls
Rose, Mr. and Mrs. Ben, 92-95
Rosenau, Mr. and Mrs. Gustave E.,
   64-67
Rudolph, Paul, 141-145
Rye, N. Y.; Franzen houses, 10-24, 54-
   59

S

San Mateo, Calif.; Jones and Emmons
   house, 198
San Rafael, Calif.; Anshen and Allen
   house, 201-203

Santa Monica, Calif.; Overpeck house,
   182-184
Sarasota, Fla.; Hiss house, 122-125
   Rudolph house, 141-145
Schaffer, Mr. and Mrs. Franklin E.,
   76-78
Schweikher and Elting, 80-83
Screen; Shoji, 65, 168-169
Screened porch, 126, 138
Seattle, Wash.; Kirk house, 167-169
Serulnic, Mr. and Mrs. George,
   158-161
Sherwood, Mills and Smith, 50-53
Shoji screens, 65, 168-169
Shreveport, La.; Wiener and Wiener
   house, 145-150
Site problems, 34, 50, 158, 185, 210
Skylight; plastic, 90-91
Smerly, Irvin, 39
Smith and Williams, 210-213
Sound control, 122
Spear, Inc., 110
Speyer, A. James, 92-95
Spivak, Benjamin, 69
Sprout, E. W., 80
Stairwell, 27-28, 40, 108-109, 125, 192-
   193
Steinwachs, Alois, 127
Steel framework, 92-93, 198
Stern & Towne, 167
Storage units, 42-43
Sunken area; in bathroom, 91
   in living room, 56, *illus. 141*, 144
   play court, 26
Swimming pool; *see* Pool

T

Taylor, Mr. and Mrs. Harwood, 114-
   117
Terrace, 50-53, 62, 144-145, 200-201
   raised, 68
   see also Court; Porch
Teufel, William G., 167
Texas Society of Architects award
   winner; Bolton and Barnstone
   house, 136-140

Tigner, Ben, 154
Tilander Bros., Inc., 92
Tiller, Dr. and Mrs. Philip M., 106-109

U

Upton, Mr. and Mrs. J. T., 119-121
Utility room, 208-209

V

Van Cleve Construction Co., 136
Vogt, Ernest, 114

W

Walls; curtain, 102
   glass, 92-94, 118-121, 162-164
   enclosing lots, 118-120, 162-164, 185-
   189, 190-193
   see also Construction; Roof
Walser, Frank, 151
Wardrobe units, 42-43
Webb, Chard F., 39-43
Wenzel Co., Inc., 45
Westover, Richmond, Va., 2-3
Whelan, Joseph, Construction Co., 162
Wiener, Samuel G., 146-150
Wiener, William B., 146-150
Wiesenfeld and Hayward, 64
Willisch, Marianne, 102
Wilson & Wedekind, 171, 178
Windows, 74-75
   in floor, 109
Wood arch roof, 110
Wooley, H. L., 205
Wurster, Bernardi and Emmons, 178-
   181

Y

Yamasaki, Leinweber & Associates, 84-
   86

Z

Zion, Robert, 87